Read, write, Play, Learn

Literacy Instruction in Today's Kindergarten

Lori Jamison Rog

INTERNATIONAL
Reading Association
800 BARKSDALE ROAD, PO BOX 8139
NEWARK, DE 19714-8139, USA
www.reading.org

The International Reading Association attempts, through its publications, to provide a forum for a wide spectrum of opinions on reading. This policy permits divergent viewpoints without implying the endorsement of the Association.

Executive Editor, Publications   Shannon Fortner
Managing Editor   Christina M. Terranova
Editorial Associate   Wendy Logan
Design and Composition Manager   Anette Schuetz
Design and Composition Associate   Lisa Kochel

Cover   Design, Frank A. Pessia; Photographs, Lori Jamison Rog

Copyright 2011 by the International Reading Association, Inc.

All rights reserved. No part of this publication may be reproduced or transmitted in any form or by any means, electronic or mechanical, including photocopy, or any information storage and retrieval system, without permission from the publisher.

The publisher would appreciate notification where errors occur so that they may be corrected in subsequent printings and/or editions.

Library of Congress Cataloging-in-Publication Data

Rog, Lori Jamison.
  Read, write, play, learn : literacy instruction in today's kindergarten / Lori Jamison Rog.
     p. cm.
  Includes bibliographical references and index.
  ISBN 978-0-87207-847-5
  1. Reading (Kindergarten) 2. Language arts (Kindergarten) I. Title.
  LB1181.2.R66 2011
  372.6--dc23

                              2011028999

Suggested APA Reference
Rog, L.J. (2011). *Read, write, play, learn: Literacy instruction in today's kindergarten*. Newark, DE: International Reading Association.

To Hayden and Rachel, who will be in kindergarten before we know it, and to the lucky teachers who get to guide them on their literacy journeys

CONTENTS

ABOUT THE AUTHOR

Lori Jamison Rog is a teacher, consultant, and staff developer. She is the author of many articles and teacher's guides as well as seven books for teachers, including *Marvelous Minilessons for Teaching Beginning Writing, K–3*.

Lori has served as the K–12 literacy consultant for Regina Public Schools in Saskatchewan, Canada, as well as a reading assessment specialist with the Saskatchewan Department of Education, but the highlights of her professional career were her years as a classroom teacher for primary and intermediate grades.

Lori is an honorary lifetime member of the Saskatchewan Reading Council and a former member of the International Reading Association's Board of Directors.

She lives in a Victorian townhouse in downtown Toronto, Canada, with her husband, Paul Kropp, who writes novels for young adults.

Currently, Lori is a private educational consultant who writes professional materials for teachers and consults with school districts. She has presented at many literacy conferences, from Nova Scotia to New Zealand and San Francisco to Dublin.

Author Information for Correspondence and Workshops
Please feel free to contact Lori with inquiries about this book or about consulting or professional development. She can be reached by e-mail at ljamison@sasktel.net, and her website is www.lorijamison.com.

eaching kindergarten has never been as challenging—or as exciting—as it is today.

In 2000, I wrote a book called *Early Literacy Instruction in Kindergarten*, based on my research and experiences as a classroom teacher, district literacy consultant, and graduate student. In the last 10 years, I have worked in and visited dozens of kindergarten classrooms across North America. Much has changed. The needs and experiences of students have changed, educators' understanding of pedagogy has changed, and the expectations for what kindergarten children should be able to achieve have changed.

One thing hasn't changed, however, and that's the commitment on the part of kindergarten teachers to make their students' first foray into formal education one that is warm with acceptance and caring, busy with exploration and activity, and rich with meaning and engagement. This new book had its roots in *Early Literacy Instruction in Kindergarten* (Rog, 2001). In fact, readers will recognize some of the core ideas. But it also emerged from my experiences and research over the past 10 years; the content reflects the changes we teachers have all experienced.

This book is about good teaching. However, while kindergarten teachers have a responsibility to engage and educate the whole child, this book examines only a portion of that task: the development of literacy.

Part I, "Foundations," examines the current research behind developmentally appropriate practice and how early childhood education has evolved. We look at the changes in kindergarten children and their world as well as at what we would like all kindergarten children to know and be able to do. Finally, we focus on the qualities of an effective kindergarten literacy classroom, including play-based learning, inquiry, and student self-regulation.

Part II, "Classroom Applications," offers practical ideas and strategies for teaching. It opens with a chapter on oral-language development, and the chapters that follow in this part of the book are organized around literacy learning structures: read-aloud; shared reading; small-group reading; independent reading; modeled, shared, and interactive writing; writing workshop; and word study. The closing reflects on the increasing diversity of students in our classrooms and how to both honor and accommodate that diversity.

I hope that novice and experienced teachers, teacher leaders, and teacher educators will find ideas in this book to inspire reflection on their own practice and add to their teaching toolboxes. Let me encourage you to do something very "unteacherly" with this book: Write in it! There is space in this book to include a few teaching ideas on every topic. I hope you will use the margins to add your thoughts and ideas as you refine your own kindergarten literacy program.

I have had the good fortune to visit exemplary classrooms and work with terrific teachers from Florida to British Columbia and Nova Scotia (where kindergarten is called "grade primary") to Mexico. I have consulted in districts where kindergarten was not even considered part of formal schooling and in districts where every kindergarten classroom was subjected to a basal program so rigid that there was (officially) no room for read-alouds or writing process.

With one foot in the fascinating land of research in early literacy and one foot in the wonderful world of the kindergarten classroom, perhaps my biggest challenge is to keep my balance. Indeed, if there is an underlying theme in this book, it is *balance*: balancing play-based learning and explicit instruction; balancing child-centered and teacher-guided curricula; and balancing whole-class, small-group, and individual structures.

In this book, I have tried to offer a research-based and practical overview (peppered with a few strong opinions, politically correct and otherwise) of how best to serve our youngest learners and guide them on their journey to becoming literate citizens of tomorrow.

Acknowledgments

As always, there are many people to thank for their support and assistance in this project: all the kindergarten teachers who have shared their ideas and their classrooms, the students from whom I have learned and continue to learn, the researchers and practitioners on whose knowledge this book is based.

In addition, I would like to acknowledge those experts who gave advice and comments on portions of this manuscript:

- Donna-Lynn Galloway (curriculum consultant—kindergarten, Halton Catholic District School Board, Ontario) and Nancy Carl (coordinator of curriculum, assessment and instruction, K–5 Literacy and Early Learning, School District #43, Coquitlam, British Columbia) for their many thoughtful comments and sound advice on this manuscript and for continually reminding me that play is a child's work

- Patty Goonen (elementary writing resource teacher, Orange County Schools, Florida) for her wisdom on writing in kindergarten and beyond

- Paula Harms (Title I consultant, CESA 10, Wisconsin) and Wilfred Burton (literacy coordinator, Regina Public Schools, Saskatchewan) for helping me find the place of guided reading in the kindergarten curriculum

- Christine Thomas (instructional support teacher, Diven Elementary School, Elmira City School District, New York) on whom I can always count to try out new ideas, respond to my queries, and take a photograph when necessary

As well, I thank the teachers and administrators in kindergarten classrooms who welcomed me into their schools, shared their ideas, and allowed me to take pictures, especially:

- Jenny DaCosta (reading specialist), Lino Rodriguez (principal), and the faculty at Grand Avenue Primary Learning Center, Orlando, Florida
- Nicole Daneault and Debra Vanderwood (kindergarten teachers) and Sandra Meister (principal) at Walton Elementary School, Port Coquitlam, British Columbia
- Wanda Carmenata (instructional leader), Laurie Storch (principal), and my "trait mates" at Southwood Elementary School, Orlando, Florida
- Marie Dore and Liliana Matute (kindergarten teachers), Patricia Rumble and Melanie Scott, (early childhood educators), and Karen Dobbie, (principal) at St. Luke Catholic School, Oakville, Ontario
- Christine Thomas (instructional support teacher), Pam Davis-Webb (principal), and the teachers at Diven Elementary School, Elmira, New York

Finally, thanks to all the teachers and families who gave permission for their photographs to appear in this book, especially:

- Kathy Stayer (kindergarten teacher), Diven Elementary School, Elmira, New York
- Bethany Ledesma and Angela Meyers-Serrano, Southwood Elementary School, Orlando, Florida
- Holly Robbins, Grand Avenue Primary Learning Center, Orlando, Florida
- My grandson Hayden, his friend Ella, and his cousin Lucas
- My kindergarten neighbour Simon Kingstone, who posed for additional photos, even when it meant he had to wipe off his pirate face paint

And, of course, thank you to Paul, who is always my anchor, mentor, and best editor.

PART I

Foundations

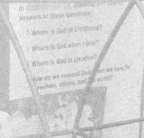

CHAPTER 1

The Changing World of Kindergarten

Long ago and far away, I went to "kindergarten" in my next-door neighbor's basement. I was a stereotypical firstborn child, and my parents sent me to kindergarten to learn to socialize (to share) and to communicate (to be less bossy). I have three distinct memories of kindergarten: competing with other kids to play with the coveted old-fashioned telephone switchboard, having to be the "fat lady" in the circus play (a trauma that will remain with me for life), and struggling to learn the difference between my right and left hands.

Some things haven't changed. As in years past, today's kindergarten is one very important beginning step in a learning adventure that will involve dozens of teachers, hundreds of peer relationships, and many different classrooms, and that will lay the groundwork for lifelong social, emotional, and cognitive health. But many things have changed in the kindergarten world.

The Experiences of Childhood Have Changed

The experiences of childhood are quite different than they were even a decade ago. The majority of kindergartners have already had some form of formal learning experiences, through child care, preschool, swimming lessons, or museum programs. Television, the Internet, and other media have produced a generation of children with wider access to their world than ever before.

> "Children entering kindergarten may be more competent and less dependent on adults than children a generation ago; more self-reliant and less interested in adult guidance; but feeling more stress and less security."
>
> *(Hatch, 2005, p. 7)*

The cultural mosaic of the children in our schools has also changed. In Toronto, where I live, 80% of children in public elementary schools have at least one parent born outside Canada. Over 50% speak a first language other than English (O'Reilly & Yau, 2009). The National Association for the Education of Young Children (NAEYC) reports that demographic trends in the United States predict "dramatic increases in children's cultural and linguistic diversity and, unless conditions change, a greater share of children living in poverty" (NAEYC, 2009, p. 2). According to the Annie E. Casey Foundation's National KIDS COUNT program (2009), 20% of children in the United States live below the poverty line. We as teachers know that these children have fewer language and literacy experiences before school and are at greater risk of learning difficulties.

There are more students in our classrooms than ever with identified cognitive, emotional, physical, and behavioral needs. These increasing populations of at-risk students have led to additional demands on schools from kindergarten onward. Schools are being held accountable for reducing the learning gaps between the rich and the poor, in spite of the many issues beyond teachers' control. As a result, we have seen numerous changes in early childhood education.

Kindergarten Structures Have Changed

In response to demands for better quality child care and more rigorous curricula in kindergarten, there has been a dramatic rise in the number of full-day kindergarten programs. Today, more than half of children in the United States attend kindergarten all day (Walston & West, 2004). Full-day kindergarten programs offer more opportunities for children to engage in meaningful learning activities. Children who attend school all day show greater gains in reading and mathematics, have better attendance, and are less likely to be retained in upper grades than children from half-day classes (Walston & West, 2004). Full-day kindergartners also exhibit more independent learning and productivity in work with others (Elicker & Mathur, 1997). In particular, at-risk students have been found to benefit most from a full-day schedule (Plucker et al., 2004).

> According to the landmark Early Childhood Longitudinal Study, children who attend school for a full day benefit socially, emotionally and academically.
>
> *(Walston & West, 2004)*

Expectations for Kindergartners Have Changed

Our expectations of what kindergartners should know and be able to do have also changed. Skills and concepts such as reciting the alphabet, counting to 10, and naming colors, once considered to be ultimate goals of the kindergarten year, are now more likely to be considered entry-level knowledge. There is now pressure on children to be able to read emergent-level texts with fluency and understanding and to compose narratives, opinion pieces, and informational texts (Common Core State Standards Initiative, 2010a).

Understandings About Teaching and Learning Have Changed

Educators have known for a long time that children are active learners who construct their own understandings about the world as they experience new things and interact with others. Jean Piaget (1929) was among the first to theorize that learning involves constantly creating and testing ideas about how the world works. As new experiences challenge these ideas, learners must either assimilate the new ideas into their existing knowledge banks or refine their existing knowledge to accommodate the new information.

When a child begins to talk, she learns very quickly what sounds generate praise and results. She may find that sounds like /wa/ or /wawa/ produce not only delight on the part of her parents but a drink of water as well. So she assimilates these sounds into her existing language repertoire. On the other hand, she may find that /gaga/, while equally delightful, does not result in a drink of water or anything else. Therefore, she must change her mindset to accommodate this new knowledge.

Children take similar steps on their journey to written language. Long before they are able to recognize actual words, they role-play reading, using illustrations and their own language repertoire and experiences to tell the story in a book (Sulzby, 1985). In writing, children begin to experiment with squiggles, which gradually become symbols and letter-like forms, before they can use conventional alphabet letters in a meaningful way (Clay, 1975).

> "Although it may seem as though some children acquire these understandings magically, or on their own, studies suggest that they are the beneficiaries of considerable, though playful and informal, adult guidance and instruction."
>
> (IRA/NAEYC, 1998, p. 198)

Learning to talk may seem like the most natural process in the world, but as children experiment with oral language, they constantly receive both incidental and intentional feedback that helps them learn to speak. The importance of modeling and feedback is why it is not enough to simply surround children with books and assume that they will learn to read and write. Modeling and feedback are what creates readers.

The interactions around print with adults and other significant people in their lives have a powerful impact on children's literacy development (Hiebert & Raphael, 1998). Among those significant people are their kindergarten teachers. While Piaget examined the natural development of children making sense of their world, Russian psychologist Lev Vygotsky (1978) went a step further by exploring the role of scaffolding in accelerating the transition from one developmental stage to another. Scaffolding is instructional support that nudges a child from what he can do on his own today to what he will be able to do tomorrow. The role of scaffolding is to "move ahead of development and pull it along" (McGill-Franzen, 2006, p. 58).

> "The window into the developing brain allows us to see that stimulation from the environment changes the very physiology of the brain, with implications for cognitive, social, and emotional growth."
>
> (Bowman et al., 2000, p. 58)

Current brain research suggests that learning patterns may be much less genetically predetermined and more affected than environmental influences than previously thought (Bowman, Donovan, & Burns, 2000). Although we must be cautious about directly applying neuroscience to teaching and learning, this research does seem to confirm the importance of a learning environment full of rich experiences, purposeful modeling, and guided exposure to complex thinking (Bowman et al., 2000).

All these factors have had an impact on the way kindergarten classrooms are structured and how kindergarten children are taught. Over the years, kindergarten teachers have been riding a virtual pendulum of teaching philosophies. As one long-time kindergarten teacher expressed to me,

> When I first started teaching, it was all about socialization and play. Our classrooms were filled with puzzles and blocks and dress-up costumes. Sure, we read books to the kids but we never expected them to read the books on their own. Then we were told to put away the toys and focus on academic standards. We weren't even allowed to have playdough in the literacy centers. Everything had to be curriculum-based, but the only curriculum that mattered seemed to be literacy. Now, we seem to be back to play again. I don't know which end is up. I keep waiting for the pendulum to swing again and hit me on the head.

Kindergarten teachers still find themselves caught in the tension between the "child-centered" and "academically-oriented" philosophical camps. *Eager to Learn*, the report of the Committee on Early Childhood Pedagogy of the National Research Council (NRC; 2001) reports that no one curriculum or pedagogical approach has been identified as superior. Certainly, there is general agreement that over-reliance on didactic practices, in which children receive extended whole-group instruction on isolated skills and pencil and paper tasks, are not appropriate for kindergarten. Play is the primary means by which young children make sense of their world. It's essential to build many opportunities for play-based learning into the kindergarten program. However, some teachers are receiving erroneous messages that a play-based philosophy means that code-related literacy activities and explicit instruction are developmentally inappropriate. Judith

Schickedanz (2004) cautions that certain foundational literacy concepts, such as letter names or beginning and ending sounds, are not "discoverable" and must be taught. However, these episodes of direct teaching should be brief, contextualized within the reading and writing processes, and as active and experiential as possible.

As the NAEYC (2009) states in its most recent position statement on developmentally appropriate instruction, teaching doesn't need to be either/or. In her doctoral dissertation, Jennifer Russell (2011) set out to explore the balance between "academic" learning models (teacher-directed instruction on discrete skills with plenty of repetition and review) and "developmental" models (learning environments that encouraged exploration and discovery) in kindergarten classrooms. What she found was that the majority of activities fell somewhere in between instructional activities that focused on academic goals but employed child-centered pedagogical techniques such as experiential learning and manipulating concrete materials.

This is why the kindergarten program must provide a balance of play-based learning and explicit instruction. A program that focuses entirely on unstructured play may not provide the foundations many children need for learning to read and write, especially those who arrive at school without rich literacy experiences. On the other hand, an emphasis on skill mastery can undermine both the developmental nature of learning and the diverse needs of students. While students may learn some literacy basics, they may miss opportunities to construct their own ideas about the world through playful interaction with print and with others.

An effective kindergarten program is structured in such a way as to respect the learning processes of all students and help them reach their full potential. It acknowledges that children will be at different stages of development and will require different instructional strategies. At its heart is a teacher who has thorough knowledge of the curriculum, the learning process, and the children involved. With this knowledge, the teacher can set appropriate learning goals to meet the needs of the students and to guide instruction. It is these challenging but achievable goals that are the essence of today's kindergarten.

CHAPTER 2

Developmentally Appropriate Practice: Look How Far We've Come

If we could travel in time back to Germany in the mid-19th century, we might have the opportunity to shake the hand of Friederich Froebel, the man who invented kindergarten. Froebel first conceived of early childhood education as a garden where young children could learn through play and activity. His "children's garden" focused learning around three areas: (1) toys such as building blocks for self-directed play, (2) singing and dancing for healthy activity, and (3) outdoor gardening for exploring the natural world (Wollons, 2000).

Throughout much of the 20th century, kindergarten instruction was influenced by the work of John Dewey, who believed that a classroom based on integrated themes helped provide meaning and purpose for children's learning (Puckett & Diffily, 2004), The dramatic play, construct-and-create, and discover-and-explore centers found in so many kindergarten classrooms today are the result of Dewey's influence.

For most of the history of kindergarten, it was not an expectation that children would learn to learn to read and write. From about the 1930s to the 1980s a philosophy of reading readiness dominated kindergarten instruction. Based on the principle that certain developmental markers must be mastered before reading can take place, reading readiness advocates believed that it was not just unnecessary, but even damaging, to try to teach children to read before they were ready. That magical moment of readiness was determined to be six-and-a-half years of age, based on the results of the 1931 reading assessments in Winnetka, Illinois, USA (Morphett & Washburne, 1931). Therefore, actual reading instruction didn't begin until the midpoint of the first-grade year, and, until that point, children were subjected to a range of exercises involving directionality, visual and auditory discrimination, and letter work—anything but books.

> Children were not thought to be ripe for reading until they had a mental age of six and a half years, and it was considered "futile if not deleterious" to try to teach children to read before they were ready.
>
> *(Hiebert & Raphael, 1998, p. 5)*

In the mid-1960s, a reading revolution burst on to the scene. In 1967, New Zealand researcher Marie Clay conducted an extensive study of the early reading behaviors of five-year-old kindergarten students, concluding that even young children could engage in some reading behaviors such as recognition of letters and words, voice–print matching, and self-correction. These were radical thoughts in an era when it was believed that reading instruction before the age of six-and-a-half years was considered to be "futile if not deleterious" (Hiebert & Raphael, 1998, p. 5).

Clay's were not the only studies of early literacy that postulated that literacy development begins long before formal instruction in school. Jerome Harste and his colleagues (Harste, Woodward, & Burke, 1984) found that children as young as three could identify labels on food packages and street signs in their environments. It would seem that the idea that symbols represent ideas would be a prerequisite for understanding that marks on a page represent words that you read.

Perhaps, suggested Clay (1966), making letter-sound connections is not the entry point into reading but a later step in a progression of behaviors leading to making meaning from print. In her 1966 doctoral dissertation, Clay coined the term *emergent reading behaviour* to define the ongoing and developmental process of understanding and using written language from birth until independence.

> "There is nothing in this research that suggests that contact with printed language forms should be withheld from any five-year-old child on the grounds that he is immature."
>
> *(Clay, 1967, p. 24)*

Emergent Literacy: What We Know Now

It's now generally recognized that children know about and participate in the functions of literacy long before they can discriminate between letters or recognize correspondences between symbols and sounds (Figure 2.1). Literacy is emerging from the time

Figure 2.1
Literacy Begins to Emerge Long Before Children Enter School

that a child recognizes that the golden arches represent a fast food chain or that the octagonal red sign tells Mom to stop the car. At a very young age, toddlers can identify their favorite breakfast cereal in the grocery aisle, or the toothpaste tube by the bathroom sink, or the name of a store they visit regularly. (Should we be surprised that the first word our grandson recognized was *Toyota*, which is his dad's employer?)

It is not uncommon to see lists, letters, stories, and maps created by children who are not yet in school (Figure 2.2). Literacy is also developing when a child insists that the scribbles on his paper say, "Grandma is coming," or "This is what I want Santa to bring." When a child recognizes that symbols can have meaning, he has tools for reading. When he uses symbols to represent his ideas, he is a writer. In fact, Susan Neuman and Kathy Roskos (1998) have suggested that the term *emergent* may be inappropriate because it implies that literacy has a beginning point. They suggest that *early literacy* is a more suitable term to describe a process that is "ongoing and continuous throughout a lifetime" (p. 2).

Most children go through similar stages as they develop reading and writing proficiency (International Reading Association [IRA]/NAEYC, 1998). However, not all

Figure 2.2
Preschoolers Often Use Pictures and Symbols to Tell a Story

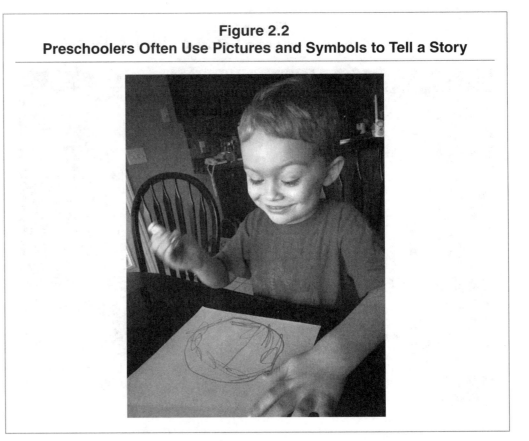

children reach each phase of development at the same time and pace. Early experiences with print play a significant role in literacy development (Adams, 1990), both in determining a child's literacy level when entering kindergarten and in defining attitudes toward reading and learning.

Meet Dakota and Mikiel, two children who attend the same kindergarten class but come from quite different literacy backgrounds: Dakota lives with her grandmother in an apartment not far from the school. Dakota's grandmother works long hours as a waitress in the local coffee shop and has little time for reading and writing. Occasionally, when she's not too tired, she will tell Dakota a traditional story at bedtime. Most of the time, Dakota and her grandmother watch television together.

> Children who are read to at home have 1,000–1,700 hours in literacy experiences before they even come to school.
>
> *(Adams, 1990)*

Mikiel attends the same school as Dakota. Mikiel's father, a professor, and his mother, an artist, fill their home with books. They make regular trips to the library, where Mikiel knows how to find his favorite books. Mikiel often sees his mother and father reading and writing for both professional and recreational purposes.

Although virtually all children in our society are surrounded by environmental print, some children come to school with a great deal more knowledge about how print works than others do. Marilyn Adams (1990) suggests that children like Mikiel have an advantage of over 1,000 hours more experience with print before starting school than children like Dakota. Although it may seem that these children acquire literacy understandings simply by immersion in print, in reality they have usually received a great deal of informal instruction and guidance from parents and other significant people in their lives (IRA/NAEYC, 1998). Dolores Durkin's (1966) classic research of children who learned to read before coming to school reveals certain patterns in their home literacy experiences. She found that when the parents of these children read aloud, they would discuss the story, point out words and other features of print, respond to the child's questions, and share in various other literacy activities such as letter writing and noting environmental print (Figure 2.3).

> "Failing to give children literacy experiences until they are school-age can severely limit the reading and writing levels they ultimately attain."
>
> *(IRA/NAEYC, 1998, p. 197)*

These interactions with others around print have the greatest impact on literacy development (Hiebert & Raphael, 1998). Therefore, it is important for both parents and teachers to be active participants in their children's and students' literacy development long before conventional reading begins.

Developmentally Appropriate Practice

Kindergartners—and for that matter, all children—are best served by teaching that is appropriate to their age and developmental stage and sensitive to their uniqueness as individuals. Just as physical growth is developmental, so is intellectual growth. The teacher's job is to set learning goals that are both challenging and attainable for students

Figure 2.3
A Mother Reads to Her Child at Home

and then to support and guide them as they progress toward those goals. This is the core of the developmentally appropriate curriculum (IRA/NAEYC, 1998).

At its foundation, developmentally appropriate practice is simply good teaching. It is instruction that honors each child's stage of development and is geared to meeting each student's social, emotional, and cognitive needs. According to the NAEYC, developmentally appropriate practices are those that meet each child where he or she is, and scaffold the child to higher levels of achievement. However, over the years there has been controversy over just what these practices should look like.

In 1986, the NAEYC released its initial position statement on developmentally appropriate practice (DAP) in an effort to consolidate the rapidly emerging research on early literacy for teachers. This position advocated a child-centered, play-oriented environment that provided children with opportunities to explore literacy—if they chose to—with little explicit teaching or intervention. Some researchers determined that students in these types of early learning experiences were more motivated and more confident about their own abilities (Stipek, Feiler, Daniels, & Milburn, 1995) and demonstrated higher achievements in later grades (Marcon, 2002). Others argued that the research supporting DAP was flawed and found no evidence that DAP affected either social or academic outcomes (Van Horn, Karlin, Ramey, Aldridge, & Snyder, 2005).

Prompted by a changing world of student demographics, expectations for student and teacher performance, and concern for children at risk of academic failure, the NAEYC issued a third edition of its position statement on DAP in 2009. While maintaining its original belief in a constructivist, child-centered philosophy, the NAEYC (2009) also acknowledges in this position statement the need for a balance of explicit instruction and modeling of critical skills.

In today's kindergarten, it is generally agreed that children need more than just incidental experiences with print. The National Reading Panel (NRP; National Institute of Child Health and Human Development [NICHD], 2000) advises that reading instruction should begin as early as possible, especially for children who have not had many experiences with print before starting school. In a major longitudinal study, Ralph Hanson and Diane Farrell (1995) followed 4,000 students in 10 states who had been taught to read in kindergarten. In their senior year of high school, these students demonstrated superior adult reading skills and habits, higher grades, and better attendance at school than their peers who had not received reading instruction in kindergarten—in spite of the fact that they represented lower socioeconomic and parent education demographics than the comparison groups.

The foundation of NAEYC's (2009) position on DAP is based on three key principles: (1) informed decision making, (2) challenging but achievable goals, and (3) intentional teaching. Decisions that guide DAP should be based on what is known about child development and learning, about the individual child, and about the social and cultural contexts the child inhabits. Effective instruction starts with what children know and can do and stretches them to higher levels of achievement, while providing adequate support to make the learning goals achievable. Finally, a critical aspect of DAP is intentionality. From organizing the classroom environment to planning instruction, the teacher's actions are always purposeful and focused on student learning.

An effective teacher is always at the core of developmentally appropriate classroom. Exemplary teachers do the following:

- Create a "caring community of learners" (NAEYC, 2009, p. 16) in which children have positive, supportive relationships with one another and with the teacher

- Acknowledge the importance of families as partners in the children's learning

- Maintain positive lines of communication

- Demonstrate respect for differing cultural and social home environments

- Use ongoing assessment to inform instruction and guide planning
- Set goals for learning that are developmentally appropriate and challenging but achievable and use these goals as a framework for a coherent and carefully sequenced set of learning experiences that start with where children are and what they know
- Have a repertoire of strategies, offer a balance of whole-class, small-group, and individualized learning and make adjustments to ensure that all children learn
- Are intentional in everything, from the classroom culture to the curriculum, guided by what their children need to know and how best to teach it

Good teachers are professionals who understand child development, pedagogy, and their own students. External programs or curricula that permit no latitude or teacher decision making undermine all that we as educators know about individual learning and differentiation.

> "The acts of teaching and learning are too complex and individual to prescribe a teacher's every move in advance. Children benefit most from teachers who have the skills, knowledge and judgment to make good decisions and are given the opportunity to use them."
>
> *(NAEYC, 2009, p. 5)*

Today's developmentally appropriate classroom is likely to include a balance of explicit teaching and exploratory play. The classroom is full of print and literacy artifacts that children are encouraged to explore. There are many opportunities for children to interact, converse, plan, and problem solve with the teacher and with one another. Children are engaged in a range of whole-class, small-group, and individual activities designed to meet their diverse needs and instructional goals.

The NAEYC's position statement (2009) reminds us to think of developmentally appropriate instruction not as either/or but as both/and. Children must have *both* explicit instruction *and* opportunities for exploration and discovery. They benefit from *both* teacher-directed activities *and* spontaneous play. They thrive on *both* opportunities for choice *and* parameters for accepted behavior. They need *both* a positive self-image *and* a healthy respect for others who may be different from them.

Dorothy Strickland (2008), a member of the National Early Literacy Panel (NELP), supports "promoting peaceful coexistence between developmentally appropriate practice and the need to address the achievement gap" (p. 1). According to Strickland, there are four key characteristics of developmentally appropriate teaching in today's kindergarten classroom:

1. It must be engaging; motivation is critical for learning.
2. It must be scaffolded, using a gradual release of responsibility in which the teacher models, then guides and scaffolds, then supports and monitors the students as they work independently.
3. It must be differentiated, stretching each child from where he or she is to where he or she can be.
4. It must involve explicit teaching, with opportunities for follow-up practice.

Reading is a cyclical and cumulative learning process: The more children read, the better readers they will become; the better readers they are, the more they are likely to read. Research has shown that reading achievement is highly affected by the frequency, amount, and diversity of reading activity (Wigfield, 1997). Therefore, it is important that kindergarten teachers work to immerse their students in books and other print and instill in their students a love of literacy and a desire to read.

The skills and attitudes that children acquire in kindergarten will have a significant impact on their learning in years to come. There needn't be a chasm between joyful learning environments in which students feel confident about taking risks, are empowered to make decisions about their own learning, and have opportunities to interact with others, and intentional, systematic instruction in the skills and strategies of literate and numerate citizens.

To quote Anne McGill-Franzen (2006),

> If we are to improve literacy, ...we all have to embrace the belief that teaching reading to 5 year olds can be a school experience that's every bit as playful, imaginative, inquiry-driven and developmentally appropriate as anything John Dewey or Jean Piaget might have dreamed up. (p. 16)

CHAPTER 3

What Do Kindergartners Need to Know?

Children enter kindergarten with an incredible diversity of experiences with literacy and print. In fact, the students in an average kindergarten class are likely to represent a developmental range of up to five years (IRA/NAEYC, 1998). Some children have been read to since they were in utero, their short lives replete with books, stories, and language. Some children are just learning to speak English and may have cultural and literacy experiences not traditional in North American classrooms. Some children are dealing with cognitive, physical, or emotional challenges that make language and learning difficult. Of particular concern are children in poverty, whose families may struggle so much with day-to-day existence that there is little energy left over for language development. We as educators know that, regardless of their innate intelligence, these children are likely to have heard fewer words and participated in fewer conversations than their more advantaged peers. Kindergarten teachers must reach and teach them all.

Given this diversity of starting points, what foundational knowledge do we teachers want our kindergarten students to have to be successful readers and writers? According to the seminal work *Preventing Reading Difficulties in Young Children* (Snow, Burns, & Griffin, 1998) and the more recent synthesis of the research on early literacy instruction conducted by the NELP (2008), it is possible to identify specific areas of knowledge that predict future literacy success. This chapter takes a look at six of them:

> "Language is unique among precursor abilities in its pervasiveness for both early and later reading competencies and for the duration of its effects on reading comprehension as code breaking turns into meaning making."
>
> *(Dickinson, Golinkoff, & Hirsh-Pasek, 2010, p. 308)*

1. Oral language and vocabulary development
2. Phonological awareness
3. Concepts of print
4. Letter names
5. The alphabetic principle (phonics)
6. Name writing

Oral Language and Vocabulary Development

A strong oral-language base is the foundation for learning to read. Unlike mature readers, beginning readers can't read words that they don't already know. Understanding how language works and how letters are strung together helps children decode and spell words. Through listening to and participating in conversations, and by asking questions and hearing answers, children learn about language, literacy, and the world.

At home, children learn to talk. At school, they must also talk to learn. Schools must help children build the vocabulary they need to express their ideas and questions as well as develop an understanding of the sounds and structures of English. Hearing modeling of adult speech, having opportunities to talk with others, and having frequent exposure to books help most children develop these important concepts.

It is widely agreed that a rich vocabulary is critical to literacy develop-ment. Research suggests that the speaking vocabulary of children entering first grade predicts not only their word reading ability at the end of that grade (Sénéchal & Cornell, 1993) but is even linked to their reading comprehension in 11th grade (Cunningham & Stanovich, 1997).

> "A well-developed meaning vocabulary is prerequisite for fluent reading, a critical link between decoding and comprehension."
>
> *(Joshi, 2005, p. 209)*

In order to learn a new word, children need many exposures to it in a variety of different contexts (Biemiller, 2004). Isabel Beck and her colleagues (Beck, McKeown, & Kucan, 2002) advocate *analytic* vocabulary instruction, which includes clear explanations and definitions of new words, along with opportunities for students to analyze, use, and compare the words. From their work with prekindergarten, kindergar-ten, and first-grade students, Connie Juel and Rebecca Deffes (2004) recommend draw-ing students' attention to the sounds and visual features of new words, as well as providing opportunities for active analysis of meaning and context, a process they call *anchored word instruction* (more information about this approach may be found in Chapter 5). Assessing vocabulary is difficult, especially for prereaders. Generally, the same techniques used to teach vocabulary may be used to assess it. Cloze exercises, in which students must fill in missing words in a piece of text, can indicate both reading comprehension and vocabulary knowledge. The Peabody Picture Vocabulary Test, probably the best known standardized measure of receptive vocabulary, is an individually administered test that requires the student to select the picture (from a set of four) that best matches a given word. However, oral-language development can be assessed quite informally, using a checklist such as the one in Figure 3.1, during teacher–student interactions.

> Additional research and teaching practices for developing oral language may be found in Chapter 5.

Phonological Awareness

Phonological awareness is the understanding that words are made up of sounds. The English language has three basic phonological (sound) units: syllables, rimes, and pho-nemes. The largest and most easily recognized sound components in words are syllables; most children can hear that the word *happy* has two parts or that *book* has one. A rime is a vowel and all the letters that follow it in a syllable, such as *-ing* or *-ack*. Initial sounds, or *onsets,* are attached to most rimes to form words, such as in *sing* or *back*. Words with the same rime rhyme, as in *sing* and *bring*. The smallest units of sound in words are called phonemes. Usually phonemes are associ-ated with individual letters, such as /m/, or digraphs, such as /th/. Often the

> The English language has three basic phonological units: syllables, rimes, and phonemes.

Figure 3.1
Oral-Language Checklist

Behaviors
☐ Uses appropriate volume and tone of voice
☐ Takes turns when speaking
☐ Stays on topic
☐ Asks questions
☐ Attends to other people speaking
☐ Uses language to solve problems or get help

Vocabulary
☐ Names colors, numbers, and familiar objects
☐ Uses vocabulary appropriately for purpose and audience
☐ Describes objects
☐ Compares and categorizes groups of objects or ideas
☐ Retells parts or all of a story read aloud, using vocabulary from the story
☐ Understands and uses common prepositions
☐ Gives and follows directions

Language Structures
☐ Can use conjunctions (*and, so, because, if*)
☐ Often speaks in complete sentences
☐ Generally speaks with grammatical correctness

Speech Sounds
☐ Articulates speech sounds correctly
☐ Speaks clearly and fluently

---

terms *phonological awareness* and *phonemic awareness* are used interchangeably; however, *phonemic awareness* refers to an ability to hear and manipulate phonemes, while *phonological awareness* is a more inclusive term that encompasses phonemes as well as larger units of sound such as syllables and rimes. The ability to hear sounds within words and to segment, blend, and manipulate those sounds is strongly correlated with success in reading (NELP, 2008) as well as writing.

The NRP (NICHD, 2000) reported that phonemic awareness is most effectively taught in conjunction with letter-sound relations. For example, when children are encouraged to stretch out the sounds in words and represent each sound with a letter or group of letters, a practice known as *invented spelling*, it helps them become better conventional spellers (Ahmed & Lombardino, 2000). As well, Jane Braunger and Jan Lewis (2006) recommend that phonemic awareness be developed by games that play with language, opportunities for sociodramatic play, and engaging in rich read-alouds and shared reading experiences.

The following types of instruction support development of phonemic awareness:

• Language play
• Sociodramatic play
• Read-alouds
• Alphabet centers and word walls
• Language experience charts
• Invented spelling

(Braunger & Lewis, 2006, pp. 83–84)

It's important to remember that 80% to 85% of students develop this understanding by the middle of first grade simply by living in a world of language (IRA, 1998). As with every other aspect of teaching and learning, we teachers need to assess what our students know so we can plan the instruction that best meets their needs. The Yopp-Singer Test of Phonemic Segmentation is a widely used individual assessment of students' ability to segment common words into their constituent sounds. For those students in need of an extra dose of phonemic awareness instruction, the NRP (NICHD, 2000) recommends small-group instruction for about 30 minutes a day for a maximum of 20 hours. In school terms, that's only two months, even in kindergarten.

> Additional research and teaching practices for developing phonological and phonemic awareness may be found in Chapter 5.

Concepts of Print

One of the first things kindergartners learn as they experiment with letters and words is that print carries a message. At first, most children are unaware that print says the same thing every time you read it. Soon they realize, however, that print is print, whether it is written with a crayon or a paintbrush, whether it is scribbled on a wall, published in a book, or stenciled on a T-shirt. Print can appear by itself or with pictures. *C-o-w* can be handwritten, printed in italics, or printed in ALL CAPS, and it still is read as *cow*. Some children grasp this intuitively; for others this concept must be explicitly taught.

Eventually, children must learn that print corresponds to speech, word by word, which is another developmental milestone. What makes this concept difficult, of course, is that we generally don't speak in individual words; we speak in streams of words. Conventions about print go back to the origins of the language. For instance, English print is read from left to right and top to bottom, and pages in a book are read from front to back, not the other way around. Mastery of these basic understandings about how print is organized, also known as concepts of print, is essential to the development of reading proficiency (Clay, 1991).

Teaching concepts of print is done most effectively through modeled and shared interactions with texts. When we read a Big Book with our students or engage in an interactive writing task, we as teachers model and demonstrate these important understandings.

Children's knowledge of print concepts can be assessed quickly and informally. For example, hand a child a book turned upside down and with its cover down to see whether he or she turns it right side up to open it. Open the book to any page and invite the child to point out the "writing" and the picture, or ask the child to point out where to start reading. To assess the child's understanding of words and letters, put two blank cards at either end of a line of print and ask the child to slowly move the cards together until

> Concepts of print include the following:
> - Constancy: the understanding that print says the same thing every time you read it
> - One-to-one correspondence: recognition of the match between individual spoken words and written words
> - Directionality: understanding that English print is read top to bottom and left to right
> - Print features: the difference between print and pictures, words and spaces, uppercase and lowercase letters, punctuation marks
> - Parts of a book: identification of title, author, cover, front, and back of a book
> - Concepts of "first" and "last" or "beginning" and "ending"

only a single word (or letter) is showing. Brief interactions such as this can yield important information about a child's grasp of concepts of print.

Letter Names

Letter knowledge is considered to be one of the best predictors of early reading success (Foulin, 2005). Marilyn Adams (1990) suggests that children who can name letters automatically will have an easier time making the connections to sounds and patterns in reading and spelling than those who still struggle to remember which letter is which. Furthermore, knowing the letter names provides a foundation for the alphabetic principle because all but four of the letters in English (*w*, *h*, *q*, and *y*) have their sounds embedded in their names. Young learners who know that the name of a letter is *D*, for example, will have an easier time recalling that the letter represents the /d/ sound.

How convenient it would be if all we teachers had to do was teach the letter names and reading would follow naturally! The truth is, however, that letter-naming drills alone provide little advantage in learning to read (Hiebert & Raphael, 1998), and simply singing the alphabet song doesn't provide meaning to the letters. We see this in Big Bird's discovery of the amazing word *ab-ca-def-gi-jeckle-mi-nop-kwer-stoov-wix-iz* from the television program *Sesame Street*. Children need a range of literacy experiences to put their letter-naming knowledge to use. Instruction in letter recognition and naming should be embedded in meaningful print. When children learn alphabet letters in the context of their own names and other personally significant words, they begin to see a meaningful purpose for letters and how they fit into the puzzle of decoding and creating words.

> Additional research and teaching ideas for reinforcing letter names may be found in Chapter 12.

The NELP (2008) found that not just the ability to correctly name alphabet letters but also the speed and automaticity with which the letters are named predicts success with conventional literacy. A common tool for practicing and assessing Rapid Automatic Naming of alphabet letters is to create a grid of 25 squares, with 5 letters repeated at random 5 times each. Students point to each letter and name it as quickly as possible. Additional ideas for alphabet naming practice may be found in Chapter 12.

The Alphabetic Principle

> "To be effective, systematic phonics instruction introduced in kindergarten must be appropriately designed for learners and must begin with foundational knowledge involving letters and phonemic awareness."
>
> *(NICHD, 2000, p. 2-93)*

The *alphabetic principle* refers to the understanding that there are predictable and consistent relations between written letters and spoken sounds— the combination of letter knowledge and phonological awareness. *Phonics* is the name for the set of rules that govern how letters go together in words.

There are four basic stages of development in a child's ability to use the alphabetic principle to read words (Ehri, 1991):

1. Prealphabetic stage: The child recalls whole words as pictographs or logographs, without identifying component parts. He or she might remember *look*, for example, by the "googly eyes" in the middle.

2. Partial alphabetic stage: The child knows some letter-sound correspondences, and is likely to guess words based on a combination of context, illustration, and some letter information, usually the initial sound.

3. Full alphabetic stage: The child has a solid mastery of letters and their corresponding sounds and can decode words by blending sounds.

4. Consolidated alphabet: The child recognizes common letter sequences as patterns and chunks and can use this information for decoding.

In its meta-analysis of research on essential components of reading instruction, the NRP (NICHD, 2000) concluded that explicit and systematic instruction in phonics is critical for beginning reading. According to the NRP, kindergartners who receive systematic beginning phonics instruction—that is, teaching that follows a planned sequence of letter-sound relationships—decode better, spell better, and comprehend better than children who receive incidental phonics or no phonics instruction at all. There are four main approaches to systematic phonics instruction: (1) synthetic, (2) analytic, (3) analogic, and (4) phonics through spelling. It bears noting that the NRP found no significant advantage to any one approach.

Despite its best intentions, the NRP report (NICHD, 2000) has led to questionable practices in some districts. Even in kindergarten, many schools are adopting commercial programs with rigid sequences of instructions, mind-numbing worksheets, and often scripted instruction to ensure the teachers' "fidelity" to the program. Letter-sound instruction and practice is more effectively implemented through playful but purposeful games and activities. However, we teachers need to remember that the ability to connect letters and sounds is a means to an end, not an end in itself. Isolated skill and drill without application to connected reading and writing does little to further children's literacy development.

The NRP's report (NICHD, 2000) reminds us that "one size fits all" doesn't apply in phonics instruction any more than it does in shoe shopping (my analogy, not the NRP's). It's important to remember that kindergarten students bring a range of experiences, skills, and knowledge to the classroom, and we as teachers must do our best to differentiate instruction to meet each one's needs.

Assessments of students' understanding and application of the alphabetic principle may be conducted informally through analyzing reading miscues or invented spelling. A comprehensive phonics inventory is available at teams.lacoe.edu/reading/assessments/inven2.html.

Four Main Approaches to Systematic Phonics Instruction

1. Synthetic approaches start by teaching the individual sounds, then how to blend them into words.
2. Analytic approaches teach whole words first, then the component sounds within the words are analyzed.
3. Analogic approaches teach students to apply word parts they know to identifying and writing new words.
4. Phonics-through-spelling approaches systematically introduce letters, sounds, and patterns with immediate application in writing.

"Programs that focus too much on the teaching of letter–sound relations and not enough on putting them to use are unlikely to be very effective.... Educators must keep the *end* in mind and insure that children understand the purpose of learning letter–sounds and are able to apply their skills in their daily reading and writing activities."

(NICHD, 2000, p. 2-96)

Name Writing

What's the most important word in any child's vocabulary? His or her name, of course! For most children, their name is the first word they are exposed to as both print and spoken word, an exposure that is repeated and reinforced over and over in many different settings (Clay, 1991). Name writing teaches students to explore print, use symbols to represent ideas, connect those symbols to sounds, combine letters into words, and see words as separate entities. The NELP (2008) found a strong correlation between future success in reading and a child's ability to write his or her name or to write alphabet letters on request.

Lea McGee and Donald Richgels (1989) agree that teaching letter names and other concepts of print using children's names taps into the egocentric nature of young children, honors their existing literacy knowledge, and provides a meaningful context for developing an understanding of concepts of print. In fact, virtually every concept about letters and print may be taught through children's names.

Additional teaching ideas for using children's names may be found in Chapter 12.

Preschool children can typically recognize and label the initial letters of their own names before recognizing and labeling any other letters (Treiman & Broderick, 1998). Janet Bloodgood (1999) reports that many young learners will attempt to write their own names (as well as other important names in their world) before even acquiring general alphabet and word knowledge. Michelle Haney, Victor Bissonnette, and Kimberly Behnken (2003) found a significant correlation between kindergarten students' ability to write their own names and their ability to identify both words and nonwords.

A simple tool for assessing name writing progress is the morning sign-in sheet. Look for elements such as use of correct letters in sequence, upper- and lowercase, letter formation, and directionality.

Kindergarten Literacy Standards

At one time, the important "preliteracy" skills described in the preceding sections might have been the ultimate goal of the kindergarten program; today, they are more likely to be just the starting point. Many kindergartners actually arrive at school already having most of the predictor skills. In fact, the *Early Childhood Longitudinal Study of Kindergarten* (Zill & West, 2000) reports that two thirds of entering kindergartners already know their letters, almost a third can identify initial sounds in words, and almost one fifth can even identify ending sounds (p. 6).

When it comes to kindergarten literacy curricula, most school districts commonly have much higher expectations for the end of kindergarten. For example, the British Columbia, Canada, prescribed learning outcomes for kindergarten include the following: "Use strategies before reading and viewing to enhance comprehension, including accessing prior knowledge, predicting, making connections and asking questions"; "Use strategies during reading and viewing to monitor comprehension, including predicting

and confirming unknown words and events by using language patterns and pictures, making pictures in their heads (visualizing) and asking the question, 'Does that make sense?'" (British Columbia Ministry of Education, 2009, pp. 14–15).

In 2010, the National Governors Association Center for Best Practices and the Council of Chief State School Officers in the United States, in consultation with teachers, researchers, and school administrators, developed a set of standards (Common Core State Standards Initiative, 2010b) that "lay out a vision of what it means to be a literate person in the twenty-first century" (p. 3). The 40 standards for reading, writing, listening, and speaking in kindergarten, already adopted in 44 states, include the following:

- "With prompting and support, describe the relationship between illustrations and the story in which they appear (e.g., what moment in a story an illustration depicts)" (p. 11).

- "With prompting and support, identify basic similarities in and differences between two texts on the same topic (e.g., in illustrations, descriptions, or procedures)" (p. 13).

- "Read emergent-reader texts with purpose and understanding" (p. 16).

- "Use a combination of drawing, dictating, and writing to compose narratives... opinion pieces...and informative/explanatory texts" (p. 19).

- "With guidance and support from adults, respond to questions and suggestions from peers and add details to strengthen writing as needed" (p. 19).

- "With guidance and support from adults, explore a variety of digital tools to produce and publish writing, including in collaboration with peers" (p. 19).

- "Confirm understanding of a text read aloud or information presented orally or through other media by asking and answering questions about key details and requesting clarification if something is not understood" (p. 23).

- "Determine or clarify the meaning of unknown and multiple-meaning words and phrases based on *kindergarten* reading and content" (p. 27).

- "With guidance and support from adults, explore word relationships and nuances in word meanings" (p. 27), such as sorting common objects into categories, relating familiar words to their opposites, and distinguishing shades of meaning among verbs describing the same general action.

There is no question that the demands on the youngest learners are greater than ever. The remaining chapters in this book explore further the best

> "I expect that what they learn in kindergarten will move them closer to becoming effective communicators, capable of full participation in the demands of social and economic life in the twenty-first century. Some kindergartners will learn to read. All will move forward in their reading development."
>
> *(Hatch, 2005, p. 29)*

practices for helping our students achieve these goals. Not all students will achieve the lofty goals set out by the Common Core Standards (Common Core State Standards Initiative, 2010a), but our responsibility as teachers is to take every child from where he or she is today to where the child has the potential to be.

CHAPTER 4

Elements of an Effective Kindergarten Classroom: Learning Through Play and a Print-Rich Environment

• • • • • • • • • • • • •

When the students in Ms. Kline's kindergarten class arrive at school, they follow predictable routines. Each one greets Ms. Kline at the door with his or her choice of a signature handshake; right now the high five and the "butterfly" handshake (see Figure 4.1) are greetings of choice. They sign in on the attendance sheet and then go to the classroom book nook, where they browse through books until class begins.

The bell rings and Ms. Kline plays a good-morning song, a signal for the group to gather for morning meeting, which is a time for establishing community and setting a context for the day. Ms. Kline chooses the name of one student to become leader of the day. The leader chooses a greeting or name game, such as the song "If Your Name Begins with B, Clap Your Hands," to welcome everyone to the day. Then they spend a few minutes focusing on the letters in the leader's name, which is added to the name wall, where it can be compared with other names and used as a reference point for alphabet play.

Ms. Kline likes to start every day with a read-aloud. Today's story is an old friend for the students, so they frequently chime in as she reads. Because they are already familiar with the story, Ms. Kline decides to play with the words, inviting the students to correct her if she makes mistakes. The children laugh as she substitutes *hat* for *bat* and *norse* for *horse*. Little do the children realize that, with this game, Ms. Kline is helping them learn to be strategic readers by monitoring their own comprehension. She often uses the read-aloud time to model important comprehension strategies such as asking questions or making connections.

If time permits, the morning meeting also includes a morning message or a daily word warm-up, in which children might be invited to share news, describe a picture, figure out rhyming riddles, or brainstorm with a partner.

Figure 4.1
Hayden and Ella Demonstrate the Butterfly Handshake

During the literacy block, Ms. Kline makes sure to provide a balance of whole-class, small-group, and independent activity. As students work and play in independent centers, she works with individuals or small groups on reading and writing development. Because Ms. Kline spent a lot of time at the beginning of the year establishing routines for independence, by now the children can move smoothly and purposefully to their chosen tasks. She may pull the whole group together at some point for a whole-group shared reading, read-aloud, or writing minilesson, then disperse them again to independent learning.

As the literacy block comes to a close, Ms Kline invites the students to reflect on their independent explorations and conducts a brief shared reading lesson on the poem of the week, during which children are invited to hunt for "twin" words and letters and build "rhyming ladders" from the words in the poem. The literacy block often ends with a writing workshop, which includes a modeled, shared, or interactive writing activity, followed by independent writing on self-selected topics.

After this block of academic focus, the children then have opportunities for active play, preferably outdoors, if weather permits.

The numeracy block follows recess. Ms. Kline usually gathers the students together as a whole group first to count the calendar, have a minilesson on a mathematical concept, and figure out a problem of the day. Once again, the students disperse to centers, enabling their teacher to work with individuals and small groups, make observations, and interact with the students.

The afternoon is divided among "special" classes such as music, art, or gym as well as explorations, which involve children engaging in self-directed inquiry activities related to a curriculum-based topic or subject.

Before the children go home, they take a few minutes to reflect on what they've learned in the day, get their take-home reading books ready, sing a farewell song, and individually say good-bye to Ms. Kline before heading out the door. Another day in the "kinder garden" is done.

• •

As in Ms. Kline's classroom, effective kindergarten programs reflect a smooth blend of predictable routines, explicit instruction, and student engagement. (See Figure 4.2 for a sample full-day kindergarten schedule and Figure 4.3 for a similar schedule adapted for a half-day program.) Hers is first and foremost a child-centered classroom; sometimes this means she provides modeling and demonstration, sometimes it means she sets the stage for guided discovery, and sometimes it means she offers the students free and independent exploration. Throughout the day, children have opportunities to learn through play by constructing and experimenting and by interacting with one another and with the teacher. Ms. Kline has created a carefully planned

Figure 4.2
Sample Full-Day Kindergarten Schedule

8:00 – 8:30	Children arrive at school and browse books
8:30 – 9:00	Morning meeting
9:00 – 10:30	Literacy block/Independent centers
10:30 – 11:00	Recess/Snack/Outdoor play
11:00 – 11:45	Numeracy block/Independent centers
11:45 – 12:30	Lunch/Outdoor play
12:30 – 1:30	Music/Art/Gym/Special subjects
1:30 – 2:30	Exploration/Inquiry
2:30 – 3:00	Afternoon wrap-up and dismissal

Figure 4.3
Sample Half-Day Kindergarten Schedule

8:00 – 8:30	Children arrive at school and browse books
8:30 – 8:45	Morning meeting
8:45 – 9:45	Literacy block/Exploration
9:45 – 10:15	Snack/Indoor/Outdoor play
10:15 – 10:45	Numeracy/Centers
10:45 – 11:15	Theme work/Inquiry/Exploration
11:15 – 11:30	Daily wrap-up and dismissal

---

environment that exposes students to many forms of text and tools for writing. She knows how to scaffold students to higher levels and how to intervene when additional support is needed. Most important, she understands and accepts the developmental nature of learning and creates a classroom that supports risk taking and individual progress.

Ms. Kline's classroom is a place where intentional teaching lives. Everything she does is geared toward making her students better thinkers, communicators, and citizens.

Teaching kindergarten has never been more exciting—or more demanding—than it is today. There is increasing pressure on kindergartners to perform and increasing pressure on teachers to ensure that they do. The children entering today's classrooms are more diverse than they have ever been—in their background experiences; their language development; their home and cultural environments; and their cognitive, physical, and emotional needs.

Many children experience a rich literacy environment long before they enter school. They have the advantage of greater vocabularies, a stronger sense of story, more concepts about print, and richer experience banks. We as educators know that children who have had frequent opportunities to read and write at home are more likely to be confident and competent readers and writers at school (Sulzby, Teale, & Kamberelis, 1989). Often when children struggle in kindergarten, it is simply because they have had limited experiences with print. Patricia Cunningham and Richard Allington (2007) remind us that thinking of these children as "inexperienced" frames their learning in quite a different way than labeling them as "delayed" or "unready."

Although few kindergarten classrooms can replicate the intimate, one-to-one connections that parents and children enjoy in a home literacy environment, there are ways to create stimulating, homelike conditions in classrooms where there is one adult to 20 or more students, who are often from very diverse backgrounds. As discussed in Chapter 2, developmentally appropriate instruction meets each child where he or she is and supports, nudges, and scaffolds him or her to higher levels of development. The key is differentiation.

In the past, the child who arrived at school already reading was relegated to the same reading readiness activities the other students were doing. The child with marginal oral-language skills might have been doomed to spend another "catch-up" year in kindergarten. Today, the child who is reading will be given opportunities to extend his or her reach as a reader, and the child who needs to catch up will receive language interventions along the way.

> Children who have had frequent opportunities to read and write at home are more likely to be confident and competent readers and writers at school.
>
> *(Sulzby, Teale, & Kamberelis, 1989)*

Exemplary kindergarten teachers are experts about child development and effective literacy practices. They are also experts about their own students, knowing exactly what strengths and needs each child brings into the classroom, and they create environments where children come first and learning is central.

There is no standard formula for what makes an exemplary kindergarten program. While each classroom is unique, research and experience inform teachers that there are many features of classrooms that work in helping children develop as literate citizens. This chapter covers only three of them: (1) play-based learning, (2) a print-rich environment, and (3) independent learning centers.

Play-Based Learning

Play is what children do for a living. Through play, they explore and make sense of their world. They interact with others and their environment. They learn to make plans, focus on tasks, take turns, solve problems, and express ideas. They communicate, collaborate, and connect with their peers. Play is probably the only activity during which children control their own environment. The NAEYC (2009) has identified the importance of play as one of the critical principles affecting child development and learning.

Play is a complex set of behaviors that seems to defy definition and explanation (Prior & Gerard, 2004). For most of us, play is simply any activity that is fun, pleasurable, enjoyable. But in the child's world, play is much more than that. It is generally agreed that important cognitive, social, emotional, linguistic, and physical skills are developed through children's play (Owocki, 1999). Creative play encourages self-expression by enabling children to interact with their environment to manipulate objects and construct creations that express their ideas, developing both gross and fine motor skills as well as

divergent thinking (see Figure 4.4). Physical play contributes to health and development by burning energy and building muscle strength. The fantasy and role-playing activities of imaginative play generate self-expression, abstract thinking, and social skills. All contribute to the development of self-regulation.

Lev Vygotsky (1978) theorized that imaginative play develops

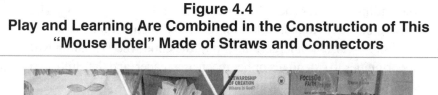

Figure 4.4
Play and Learning Are Combined in the Construction of This
"Mouse Hotel" Made of Straws and Connectors

symbolic, abstract thought, an important precursor to reading. For example, when children begin to use one object to represent another, such as pretending a big box is a spaceship, they are developing the concept of symbolism, an important concept in a world of print where ideas are symbolized by letters and words.

Free play involves choice, spontaneous decision making, and self-regulation. Structured play tends to be adult guided or rule governed, while still requiring an element of engagement and fun on the part of the players. We as teachers must make room in our kindergarten programs for both.

The play-based kindergarten curricula of the past have, in many cases, been supplanted by didactic programs that focus more on written than spoken language. Yet there are few activities that promote oral-language development better than free play. Play supports the development of the whole child, especially his or her ability to communicate, collaborate, negotiate, ask and answer questions, give and act on commands, and generally connect with others. It is important for classrooms to provide an atmosphere that encourages risk taking, a structure that provides opportunities for children to interact with each other, and an environment in which children can make choices. These are the building blocks of independent learning.

Simply giving children an opportunity to engage in free play will not guarantee that literacy will develop, however. Vygotsky (1978) also emphasized the importance of a more experienced person in the play environment; in other words, the teacher, parent, or more mature player has a key role in guiding the literacy development of children through play. Lesley Morrow and Muriel Rand (1991) found that children are more likely to engage in literacy activities during play when teachers model integrating artifacts such as books, writing tools, and signs into the play. During play-based learning, the teacher's role is first to observe and then to guide, participating in the play and intervening as appropriate to extend children's thinking or enrich their talk. A good rule of thumb is for teachers to observe for three minutes before entering into the play.

Play-based learning in today's kindergarten is not simply a return to the diversions of old, where learning was incidental and the teacher little more than a babysitter. It is carefully balanced with explicit and purposeful instruction and practice in essential skills and new learning. As the NAEYC (2009) suggests, it shouldn't have to be an either/or situation but a both/and situation. Explicit instruction and practice can coexist quite peacefully with unstructured play in the kindergarten program. We as teachers can— and should—integrate literacy behaviors into independent play by incorporating literacy artifacts such as print materials and writing tools. In Figure 4.5, a kindergartner, Michael, writes about the police station he just built. His writing, "Me and Morgan made a police station," is shown in Figure 4.6. In literacy-rich classrooms, it is an expectation that students will record their learning. In these classrooms, the teacher is constantly observing, teaching, supporting and collaborating to ensure that students are developing both

Figure 4.5
Michael Writes About the Police Station He Built With Blocks

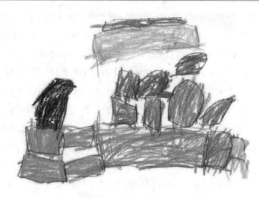

Figure 4.6
Michael's Writing About His Police Station

knowledge and self-regulation. We can also learn from the principles of play to make instruction more engaging, interesting, interactive, and rewarding for students by introducing games to play with words and sounds. We need to introduce more gross-motor movement, especially for male students. We can consider ways to make our teaching more process oriented, rather than product oriented, with activities that generate success and confidence, while stretching students to higher levels of proficiency. This is the premise behind many of the teaching ideas in this book.

Play as Inquiry or Exploration

In one classroom I visited recently, the students and teachers do not refer to *centers* or *play* but to *explorations*. The children use *tools* and *materials* rather than *toys* to conduct their explorations. This is real work as they plan, construct, evaluate, and engage. Before exploration time, the children take time to plan how they are going to use their time, and at the end of the day, they gather again to reflect on what they accomplished. This planning and reflection might be done orally in pairs, or it might be done individually on planning and review sheets such as those shown in Figure 4.7.

Joan Youngquist and Jann Pataray-Ching (2004) use the term *inquiry* to distinguish between the kind of play that children do outside school and the kind of play that exists within the educational curriculum. Like free play, inquiry should be intrinsically motivated, personally meaningful, and socially engaging to the learner. However, inquiry goes a step further than free play in that it "connotes critical and reflective thought and promotes the attainment of the intellectual capacity of every learner" (p. 46).

Popularized by the schools of Reggio Emilia, Italy, the inquiry or project-based curriculum revolves around the interests and questions of the students. As they demonstrate an interest in a topic or theme, the teacher provides supports and resources to enable them to explore and make discoveries about the theme. Books, technology, hands-on artifacts, instruments for writing and creating, and discussion and dramatic play are some of the tools with which inquiry is conducted. Students must plan their actions, gather information, and construct new ideas. They learn to communicate, negotiate, cooperate, and function independently as they explore a cross-curricular topic over an extended period of time. Meanwhile, the teacher is observing and collecting data, participating in and guiding play, and asking questions and probing thinking.

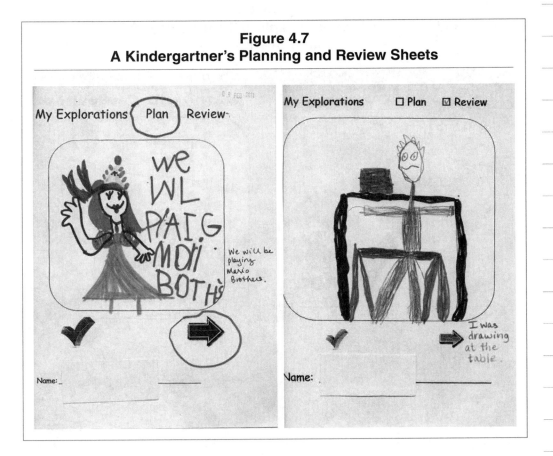

Figure 4.7
A Kindergartner's Planning and Review Sheets

Like thematic learning, inquiry offers an opportunity to teach students about new concepts and ideas that they would not be likely to discover on their own. What makes inquiry different from themes is the degree of student choice and self-regulation. With the teacher's guidance, the students decide what aspects of the topic they are interested in developing. For example, after reading Jack and the Beanstalk, one class had many questions about how tall beans really grow. Several students expressed an interest in growing bean seeds. Some wanted to cut apart a bean seed and look at it under a microscope. Others wanted to find out what plants are the tallest in the world. With the teacher's help, they conducted an Internet search, created a chart with pictures and information about some of the tallest trees in the world, and then paced out the trees' measurements on the playground. Another teacher introduced a light table to teach students about shadows and silhouettes and how light is made up of many colors (see Figure 4.8). Some students became very interested in the way colors blend and recorded their learning, such as "I mixed light blue with dark green and it made turquoise" (see Figure 4.9).

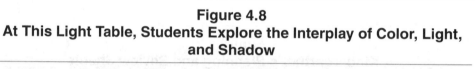

Figure 4.8
At This Light Table, Students Explore the Interplay of Color, Light, and Shadow

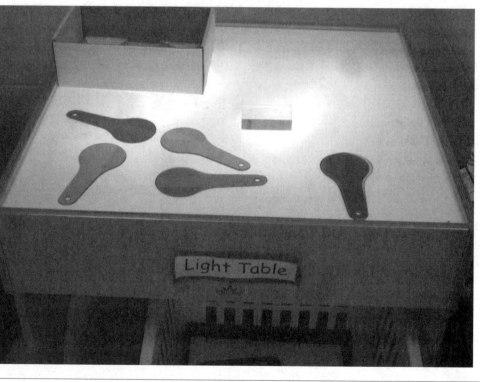

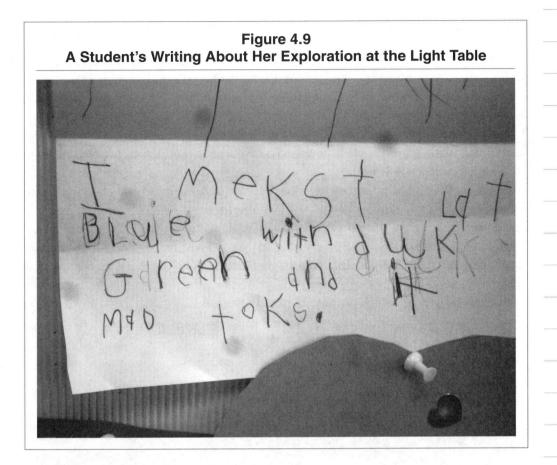

**Figure 4.9
A Student's Writing About Her Exploration at the Light Table**

While there may be certain key skills or instructional goals the teacher wants every students to learn or achieve in an inquiry project, it is not necessary for all the students to engage in the same activities. Inquiry facilitates self-direction while opening the doors to new and exciting learning in kindergarten.

A Print-Rich Environment

Careful attention to a classroom's physical design contributes to the success of a kindergarten literacy program. A classroom designed to promote optimal literacy development is full of materials to support speaking, listening, reading, and writing. It's important that books and other print materials are easily accessible to students, with items changed regularly to maintain student interest. We want students to associate literacy with pleasure and success—interestingly, the key features of play as well. Partitioning the room into small spaces helps to increase verbal interaction and facilitates cooperative activity. Small, enclosed spaces lend themselves to quiet play and talk (Roskos, 1995). Not everyone has the luxury of a reading loft, but a tent, a set of beanbag chairs, or some overstuffed pillows may be used to define the quiet reading space. Even desks, bookshelves, plants, easels, and other large objects may be strategically arranged to create boundaries in the classroom.

Literacy-rich classrooms are filled with print; books, charts, posters, signs, word walls, and other displays abound (see Figure 4.10). One of the first signs of emerging literacy in young children is the recognition of print in the world around them (Miller, 1998). They see stop signs, billboards, and names of stores and fast food restaurants. Labeling objects in the room is one form of environmental print in the classroom. It's not uncommon in kindergarten classrooms to see signs on everything from the window to the pencil sharpener.

Environmental print in the classroom enables students to behave and view themselves as readers and can be a source of meaningful print for instruction in phonetic principles. However, a label on the door is of little value if the children don't know whether the letters read *d, o, o, r* or *w, x, y, z*. To take full advantage of print-rich environments, children must interact with the print, not just look at it. It takes a teacher to draw students' attention to the print, identify letters and sounds, make connections between words, and help them see the purpose of print in their lives.

Figure 4.10
Kindergarten Classroom Walls Should Abound With Print

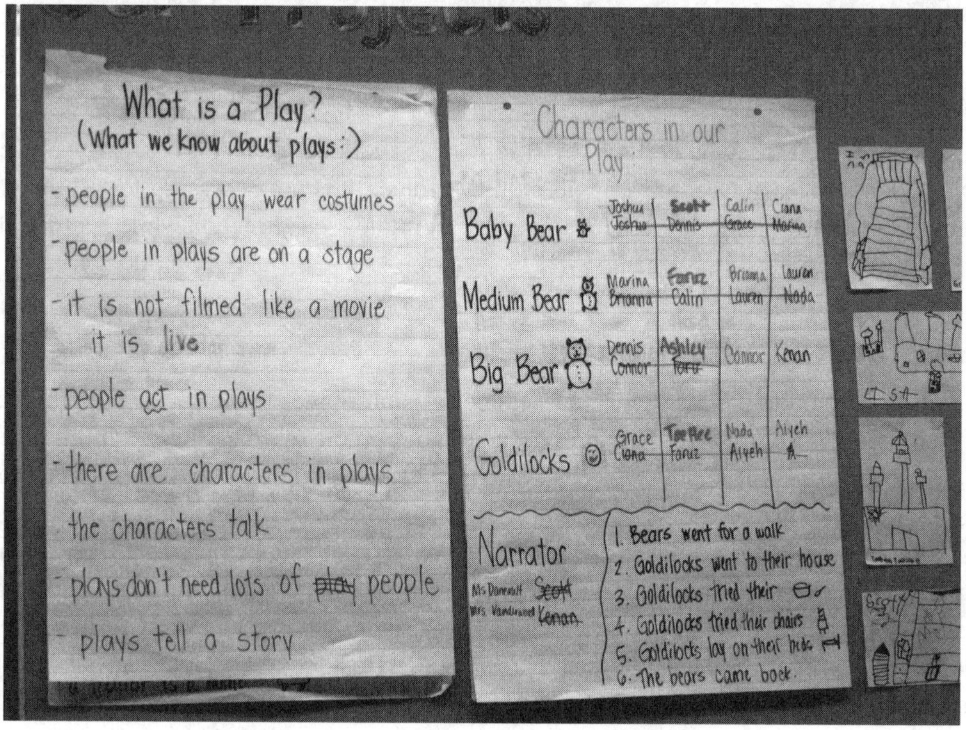

The NAEYC (2009) cautions against cluttering the environment with purposeless print that tunes children out rather than engages them. Signs and labels in the classroom should be purposeful for learning and meaningful to the students, who should have opportunities to initiate and even generate the labels for important items in the classroom. For example, students might create a label for the guinea pig's cage, along with instructions for the animal's care or a sign reminding students to be quiet in the reading corner. Students should also have many opportunities to label their own environment with their names.

> Environmental print is just wallpaper unless it is used for teaching and learning.

Independent Learning Center

Learning centers are purposefully planned classroom structures where students work with hands-on materials to guide their own learning. Centers can be an excellent means of reviewing and reinforcing previously taught concepts. They provide opportunities for individual and collaborative use of manipulatives and other materials that could not be used practically by all the students at the same time. Centers enable students to work with one another, make choices both individually and cooperatively, solve problems, practice communication, and explore their world. Most important, by providing choices that offer both success and challenge, centers can have a positive impact on students' self-regulation and motivation, which are the building blocks for independent learning.

There are four main types of centers commonly found in kindergarten classrooms: (1) literacy and numeracy centers, (2) exploration centers, (3) creativity or construction centers, and (4) dramatic play centers. Centers that focus specifically on literacy development may be found in most kindergarten classrooms today. (See the example in Figure 4.11.) Often literacy centers are the structures for independent work during small-group instruction, and students may be given the choice of which centers to visit and when, or they may be required to cycle through each center in a prescribed sequence.

The library or reading corner is likely to be a focal spot in the classroom, made inviting and comfortable with soft cushions, stuffed animals to cuddle, and, of course, collections of wonderful books reflecting a range of genres and cultures. The writing center, organized with a variety of tools for writing and paper of various sizes, shapes, and colors, is also a central feature of the kindergarten literacy program. Stickers, fancy hole punchers, and a stapler are also popular items with students, but students need to be taught how to properly use these tools before we place them in the center for independent use. Ask parents to donate old stamps and stationery, and cutting the fronts off greeting cards makes great postcards.

Other literacy centers offer whiteboards, games and puzzles, letters and other manipulatives, and e-books and websites for reading on the computer. Centers do not need to have elaborate displays or take up a great deal of space. A plastic container might hold a set of alphabet stamps and a stamp pad. An old backpack might be storage for a board game and a beach towel to sit on. Hula hoops can also define a space for center work; usually two students can sit comfortably within a hula hoop and play a game. Don't let dice

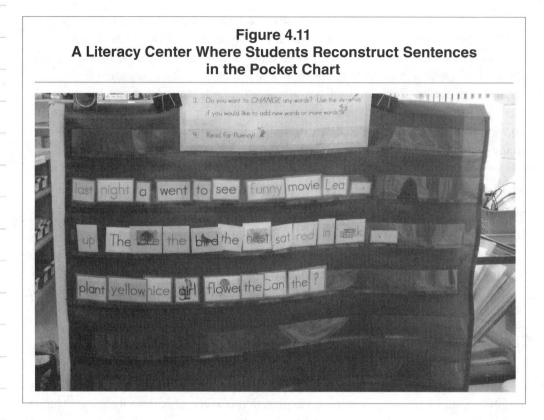

Figure 4.11
A Literacy Center Where Students Reconstruct Sentences in the Pocket Chart

roll away; put them in an empty pill container. That way, students can roll the dice within the container and look through the bottom to see the numbers. In the center in Figure 4.12, kindergartners find pictures and words in the box to sort by *ig* and *in* family words.

Sometimes called *work stations* (Diller, 2003), today's literacy centers are focused, goal oriented, and curriculum based. They should be purposeful and differentiated with learning opportunities for students at all levels, providing students with opportunities to practice and reinforce skills and concepts that have already been taught in class. These centers may be changed less frequently than traditional centers; in fact, key stations such as the reading or writing center remain in place all year, with new materials integrated into the centers to support classroom instruction. With well-organized activities and carefully established routines, learning centers can be exciting and engaging experiences that move all students toward meaningful independent learning.

In our zeal to support our students' literacy growth, we cannot ignore the important contribution that discovery and dramatic play centers make to students' social and language development. Discovery centers invite students to explore and manipulate artifacts, make discoveries, and solve problems related to a subject, theme, or inquiry topic such as seeds or dinosaurs. A discovery center might have a magnifying glass, microscope, or a collection of objects for students to sort and label, such as those seen in Figure 4.13, which invites students to contribute objects of beauty, such as colored leaves, a dinosaur

Figure 4.12
A Literacy Center Where Students Manipulate Letter Tiles to Form Word Family Words

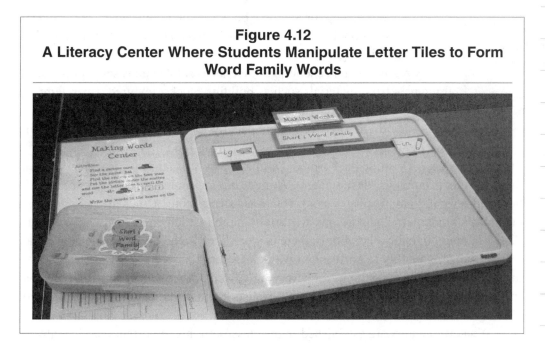

Figure 4.13
A Discovery Center Where Students Explore, Manipulate, and Read About "Beautiful Things"

As an alternative to elaborate centers, provide a "tickle trunk" with costumes, puppets, and toys to stimulate dramatic play. Even a collection of scarves can be used imaginatively for costumes.

hatching from an egg, or a child's book of Van Gogh's paintings. (Sharon Dennis Wyeth's book *Something Beautiful* would be a wonderful read-aloud addition to this inquiry.)

Creative centers encourage students to paint at an easel or craft something new from materials such as building blocks, textured paper, tempera paints, modeling, clay or the straws and connectors pictured on page 30.

Sociodramatic play centers usually focus on simulations of real-life experiences for students, such as preparing food in a kitchen, shopping at the grocery store, or visiting the hospital. Dramatic play stirs students' imaginations and facilitates their language development. At one time, a kindergarten classroom might have had several dramatic play centers such as a grocery store, a kitchen, and a hospital, but today's kindergarten classrooms are usually more restricted in time, space, and curricular latitude. In many classrooms, there is more likely to be one dramatic play center that is changed monthly to correspond with classroom themes. Creative teachers have turned spaces in their classrooms into everything from pizza parlors and barber shops to space ships and birthday parties. Figure 4.14 lists some of the many innovative center ideas teachers might use in their classrooms.

Whatever centers are established in the classroom, it's important that they always contain some "literacy artifacts" that engage children in reading and writing as part of their dramatic play (Neuman & Roskos, 1992; see Figure 4.15). For example, a

---

Figure 4.14
Innovative Center Ideas

Teachers have shared the following creative centers ideas with me:
- restaurant or pizza parlor
- various types of stores such as books or toys
- travel agency
- veterinarian's office
- barber shop or beauty salon
- video rental shop
- theater
- florist
- beach
- fix-it shop
- ice cream parlor
- spaceship
- inside of a truck
- gym
- office
- birthday party
- a classroom for playing school (believe it or not!)

Figure 4.15
A Kindergartner Writes About His Wooden Block Construction

housekeeping center might include a notepad by the telephone for taking messages, some recipes, and newspaper flyers advertising grocery sales. A pizza parlor needs menus and paper for taking orders, as well as books like *Let's Make Pizza* by Mary Hill and *Pizza Counting* by Christina Dobson. And a spaceship wouldn't be complete without a captain's log and a map of the solar system.

Managing Centers

If centers are to be meaningful learning experiences, the routines and procedures must be modeled, taught, and reinforced before students can be expected to participate in the centers independently. When learning centers are not successful, it is often because we as teachers have not taken the time to teach and practice the procedures. As with any new learning activity, center routines first must be discussed and demonstrated by the teacher. Then students need ample opportunities for guided practice before they can be expected to work independently. Take time to teach one center at a time and ensure that the students know how to conduct themselves in the center before allowing them to explore on their own.

Consider the gradual release of responsibility model (Pearson & Gallagher, 1983): I do, we do, you do. "Center school" starts with demonstrations of the activities and manipulatives in the center; then students get opportunities to explore the center under supervision. Allow those students who can work on their own to visit the center first. Then gradually allow others to join the center as they demonstrate the ability to work independently. Only when you feel confident that your students are capable of accomplishing the tasks independently should you move on to teaching another center. Remember that learning centers are not intended for teaching completely new concepts; they provide opportunities to reinforce and practice skills and strategies that have already been taught.

Establishing the necessary routines for learning activities, record keeping, movement between centers, and seeking help may take several weeks, but it is worthwhile. Taking time to teach will ensure that students gain the most benefit and motivation from the centers. Careful observation will let you know whether students need more support or whether they can move on to more complex tasks.

It is important to teach students not only how to complete the learning activities but also how to conduct themselves while in the center, how to take care of and store the materials, and how to make transitions from one center to another. Any inappropriate behavior can be minimized by establishing clear expectations and teaching routines, but it may be necessary to establish consequences for any student who disregards procedures, such as withdrawing that student from center activities. Frequent misbehavior, however, may be a sign that the center activities are too difficult or the management procedures are unclear or unsuccessful.

> Organizing the class around learning centers teaches more than literacy:
>
> "You are helping children understand how to conduct themselves as members of cooperative groups. They are learning how to fulfill commitments, manage time, manage tasks without constant reminders and supervision, conserve materials, collaborate with others, and respect others' rights."
>
> *(Fountas & Pinnell, 1996, p. 65)*

The Heart of the Kindergarten Classroom

At the heart of the effective kindergarten program is a knowledgeable, caring, and effective teacher. In an outstanding kindergarten classroom, the teacher's expertise ranges from the larger world of how children learn to read and write to the smaller world of the specific strengths and needs of his or her students. Teachers celebrate and affirm what students know and can do and at the same time extend and stretch them to higher levels of learning. In an outstanding kindergarten classroom, the teacher understands the developmental nature of learning to read and write, accepts individual differences, and adapts the instructional program to meet the needs of the students. Excellent instruction builds on what students already know and can do and develops the knowledge, skills, and attitudes necessary for lifelong learning.

The excellent kindergarten teacher is intentional, focusing on children's learning in all he or she does, from carefully planned instructional sequences to those serendipitous "teachable moments" that arise.

In their research on exemplary teachers, Cathy Collins Block and John Mangieri (2009) describe excellent kindergarten teachers as "Positive Pacers" (p. 216) whose powerful belief in their students and whose ability to adjust the pace of instruction to suit the needs of all learners generate both high expectations and high achievement.

First and foremost, however, each of us must establish a caring community of learners, a physical, emotional, and cognitive environment that is conducive to learning and growing. We can do this by establishing predictable routines, physically safe surroundings, and parameters for behavior and treatment of others. Most important, we must model empathy and caring for others. A positive relationship between the teacher and a child not only promotes learning but also supports social and emotional well-being. Children construct meaning about their world through their interactions with others and their environment and develop best when they have secure, positive relationships with responsive adults and peers (NAEYC, 2009). There is no question that teaching kindergarten is a complex juggling act that requires knowledge, skill, and true concern about the lives of the children in the class.

Classroom Applications

"Teacher, I Hurt My Arm Knee!": Oral Language, Phonological Awareness, and Vocabulary Development

When I was a literacy consultant for my district, I was often asked by parents, "What should we do to prepare our child for kindergarten?" I always told them to make sure their child could talk. In other words, encourage your child to express ideas in phrases and sentences. Help your child understand the difference between questions and answers. Read aloud and make sure he or she hears a lot of rich language.

Still, I hear from teachers all across North America that more and more children are arriving in kindergarten without strong oral-language skills. Children are having more articulation issues and more trouble communicating their ideas. Most telling, they have smaller vocabularies, especially students in communities with lower socioeconomic status. Research studies provide evidence to support these teachers' experiences. In Betty Hart and Todd Risley's (1995) classic study, they report that preschool children from affluent families are exposed to about 30 million more words than children of impoverished families. In other words, even before these children show up at the classroom doors, there is already an exponential difference in their experience with words! When my three-year-old grandson said, "Actually, Grandma, it's complicated..." I couldn't help but compare his language to the six-year-old who came to me on the playground crying, "Teacher, I hurt my arm knee," not having the word *elbow* in his vocabulary.

> **The 30 Million Word Gap!**
>
> Before they even begin school, children from professional homes have heard about 45 million words, whereas children from high poverty homes have heard only about 15 million words.
>
> *(Hart & Risley, 1995)*

We as educators know that oral language is the foundation of literacy. James Britton (1970) expressed this idea most poetically when he said, "Talk is the sea upon which all else floats" (p. 164). Why is oral language so important to beginning literacy? For one thing, beginning readers can't read words they don't know how to say. Knowing how language works and how words go together provides syntactic cueing systems to help children read and write unfamiliar words. Weak oral-language skills can have a long-term impact on children's literacy development. Laura Justice and Paige Pullen (2003) reported a significant correlation between students' vocabulary and grammar in

---

Figure 5.1
Cambourne's Conditions for Language Learning

1. Immersion in language
2. Demonstrations of literate behavior
3. Expectation that students will be able to succeed
4. Responsibility on the part of the learner
5. Encouragement of approximation as learning is constructed
6. Recognition that there is some use or purpose in the learning
7. Positive responses to student learning
8. Engagement of the learner

Note. Reprinted from Cambourne, B. (1988), *The whole story: Natural learning and the acquisition of literacy.* Auckland NZ: Ashton Scholastic.

> "Kindergarten children's performance on vocabulary (semantic) and grammar (syntax) tasks account for a significant amount of variance in later elementary grade reading ability."
>
> *(Justice & Pullen, 2003, p. 90)*

kindergarten and their reading performance in upper grades. McGee and Richgels (2003) concur: "Children with delayed spoken language development are far more likely to experience reading difficulties than children with well-developed spoken language abilities" (p. 6).

We as educators know many things about supporting oral-language development in the early childhood classroom. In fact, over 20 years ago, Brian Cambourne (1988) defined a relation between oral-language development and literacy learning, outlining key conditions under which language learning, both written and oral, is supported (see Figure 5.1). And yet, researchers such as Judith Schickedanz (2004) express concern that an emphasis on rigorous instruction and testing has caused kindergarten classrooms to focus too much on print-related activities and not enough on speech-related activities. We as teachers owe it to our students to provide an appropriate balance of both.

Oral-Language Development: Function and Form

In his book *Reading Begins at Birth*, David Doake (1988) states, "In order to learn to read as fluently and easily as they learn to talk, children have to establish control over the oral dimensions of written language" (p. 30). The NRP report (NICHD, 2000) has reminded us teachers that vocabulary development and phonemic awareness, both oral-language skills, are two of the pillars of reading instruction. However, there is much more to oral communication.

Many young children are unaware that the language people use differs according to the circumstances, audience, and purposes for which it is intended. People speak differently when they are talking to a baby than when they are presenting a paper at a university or delivering a toast at a wedding. This is the *function* of language, also known as *pragmatics*. Adults are accustomed to changes in language, style, and tone, but these subtleties often are not evident to children.

> The rules that govern social language use are called pragmatics. We use different language according to the social setting, the purpose for communication and even the relationship between the speaker and listener.

For many children, the social conventions of language need to be explicitly modeled and taught. Some of these conventions include the type of language used, tone of voice, and even such body language as gestures or the distance one speaker stands from another. (Recall the famous *Seinfeld* episode about the "close talker" who so discomfited Jerry and his friends.) While maintaining eye contact is considered important in Northern European cultures, students in some cultures (such as the students of Cree descent whom I taught in the Canadian prairies) may consider direct eye contact a sign of disrespect. It's important for us teachers to be sensitive to the languages and cultural patterns that students bring to school. Even children who speak English as their first language may come to school with different dialects or speech patterns. In 1996, for example, the Unified School District in Oakland, California, USA, mandated instruction in African American Vernacular English, known as *ebonics*. This caused a great deal of controversy among the African American community, some of whom felt that this action was patronizing to students and put them at a disadvantage for communication in the wider world. Formal patterns of language are not necessarily better, but they are different, and many students rely on school to teach them when patois is acceptable and when standard English is preferred.

> Different cultures have different language conventions, and simple gestures or tones of voice may be interpreted in diverse ways.

Students in kindergarten must learn that spoken communication changes according to the situation and the purposes for which it is used. For example, we all use different voices, and often different words, on the playground than we do in the classroom. When children understand the pragmatics of oral language, they are better able to understand that "book language" is often different from conversational language. Like oral language, the vocabulary, style, and structure of book language will differ for different types of texts.

Another important aspect of oral language is form, or *syntax*, which refers to the conventions that govern how words go together in a language. Formal grammar, parts of speech, and sentence structure are aspects of syntax. Knowledge of oral-language syntax helps readers predict unfamiliar vocabulary by giving them a sense of how the word fits into a phrase or sentence. The rules of language provide a cueing system for helping students word solve in both reading and writing. By the time children reach kindergarten, most are able to use standard language forms most of the time, although some irregular forms may appear, such as "I brang it," or "I goed there."

> Syntax refers to the conventions that govern how words go together in our language, and it includes grammar and sentence structure.

Consistent modeling and many opportunities for talk in the classroom will help all students develop critical oral-language foundations for spoken and written communication.

The most important—and perhaps easiest—ways we can help young children develop oral-language skills are to give them lots of opportunities to hear and practice talking.

Barbara Wasik (2010) offers two important suggestions for teachers:

1. Take every student response one step further by asking another question or prompting the speaker to elaborate or support his or her answer.

2. Make it a practice to expand on children's comments by restating them with more explicit and descriptive vocabulary.

Classroom talk can be the most important tool teachers have for building oral-language skills. Unfortunately, most classroom talk focuses on basic procedures or management issues. Even when discussing ideas and asking questions, teachers tend to solicit brief responses from students and rarely offer more than a few words of feedback (Wasik, 2010). Most often, the richest dialogue between teachers and students seems to occur on the playground or in the lunch room.

Susan Massey (2004) advocates purposeful planning of cognitively challenging conversation opportunities during both formal and informal instructional settings. She recommends "engaging children in conversations that involve explanations, personal narrative, and pretend play where children create and re-create events, analyze experiences, and share opinions and ideas" (p. 227). When children are asked open-ended questions and are prompted to expand and elaborate on their ideas, they develop more oral-language and vocabulary proficiency (Wasik, 2010).

Play-based learning is an important opportunity for students to engage in extended dialogue, and teachers can play an important role as collaborators in the conversations. The following learning activities, which use a range of group structures, also support language development.

Question and Answer Games

Guessing games usually involve asking and answering questions. They might include variations of "20 questions," a game in which students ask yes/no questions to guess a person, place, or thing. As a variation to the traditional show and tell, teachers can provide students with a gift bag to bring a mystery item to school. (The size of the bag effectively limits the range of items!) The leader may provide clues for the others to guess what the item is, or the students may ask yes/no questions for the leader to answer.

List and Label

Students brainstorm words to fit categories such as "things that are square," "things that have buttons," or "containers for holding things." An alternative to having students brainstorm words is to bring three common objects into the classroom and invite students to tell what they have in common. For example, I might bring in a flashlight, a light bulb, and a picture of a sun. When students can identify them as "things that make light," I will ask them to brainstorm other things that might fit into this category. You can send a note home to parents explaining this activity and inviting students to bring in their own sets of three items to categorize.

Words From Pictures is a game adapted from Emily Calhoun's (1999) Picture-Word Inductive Model. Using a picture as a prompt, students "shake out" a collection of words related to the picture. These student-generated vocabulary words are analyzed by the group for phonetic elements and are sorted in a variety of ways before being used for oral and written sentence building.

Newstelling

Daily newstelling activities help students communicate ideas and learn about the world. In some classrooms, the daily news is a collaborative event at the end of the day, during which students reflect upon what they learned and experienced that day. In others, the

daily news is a "morning meeting" activity in which one student is invited to share with the class or all students share with partners. The news is usually something the student did the night before but may be an upcoming event or even new information the student learned. This is a good opportunity to teach students the who, what, when, where, and why format for news. Encourage partners to ask at least one question about the news for the newsteller to answer.

Narratives

Narrative activities include retelling stories, creating new stories, or role-playing as story characters. This activity often occurs informally in the reading corner or dress-up center. As a more formal group activity, I might use three gift bags, with character cards in one, setting cards in another, and problem cards in another. The leader of the day draws three cards—one from each bag—and the students must collaboratively create a story that includes all three parts.

Descriptions

Teach students to describe objects or pictures by asking questions like, "How big is it?" "What color is it?" "What is it used for?" and "What are some other things that are like it?" Encourage students to use complete sentences in their descriptions and extend them by adding sensory details such as "it feels like" or "it sounds like."

Barrier Games

In this activity two students sit on either side of a barrier that prevents each of them from seeing what the other is doing. (The barrier can be as simple as a book propped up between them.) Each student has an identical set of materials. One student describes a design for the other student to re-create, such as a pattern of blocks, a simple drawing, or duplicate sets of removable stickers on a background. Based only on the description, the other student tries to create the same pattern.

Phonological Awareness: Hearing the Sounds in Words

Words are made up of sounds. The ability to hear, distinguish, and replicate the sounds in words, also known as *phonological awareness*, is a foundation on which reading is built. For young readers to learn to decode and spell words, they must hear these sound structures: syllables, rimes, and phonemes.

The largest and most easily recognized sound components in words are syllables. Most children can hear that the word *happy* has two parts or that *book* has one part. Rimes are also sound chunks that most children seem to master with ease. A rime consists of the vowel in a word and any consonants that come after it. For example, in the word *start*, the rime is *-art*. When words share the same rime, such as *cart* and *smart*, they generally rhyme. Phonemes are the smallest units of sound that can change the meaning of a word. Usually phonemes are associated with individual letters, such as /m/, or letter combinations, such as /th/ or /ea/. The phoneme that begins a syllable, such as the /c/ in *cart*, is called an onset.

> Phonological awareness encompasses a "whole spectrum, from primitive awareness of speech sounds and rhythms to rhyme awareness and sound similarities and, at the highest level, awareness of syllables or phonemes."
>
> *(Neuman, Copple, & Bredekamp, 2000, p. 124)*

Often the term *phonological awareness* is used interchangeably with the more specific term *phonemic awareness*. *Phonemic awareness* refers to an ability to hear and manipulate phonemes. *Phonological awareness* is a more inclusive term that encompasses larger units of sound, such as syllables and rhymes, as well as phonemes. Phonemic awareness abilities in kindergarten are considered to be good predictors of successful reading acquisition later in life (Adams, 1990; IRA, 1998; Stanovich, 1994).

> Although not explicitly connected to letters and print, phonemic awareness abilities in kindergarten are considered to be good predictors of successful reading acquisition.

Phonological awareness actually comprises a hierarchy of skills, with some preceding conventional reading, some developing concurrently with reading, and some acquired as a result of the ability to read, as shown in Table 5.1. The most basic levels of phonological awareness—syllabication and perception of rhyme—develop earliest and most easily. This has led some researchers to believe that an understanding of and ability to distinguish rimes and onsets is a precursor to reading (Goswami & Bryant, 1990). Intermediate-level skills such as segmenting and blending have a strong reciprocal relationship with reading; it is likely that they develop along with reading ability and facilitate decoding and spelling (Nation & Hulme, 1997).

Highest level phonological awareness tasks such as phoneme deletion and manipulation are generally unattainable by children who have received no formal reading instruction (Adams, 1990; Peterson & Haines, 1992). Think about the mental processes involved in removing the /d/ from *card* and replacing it with /t/ to make *cart* or changing the /a/ in *card* to /o/. According to Adams (1990), the ability to delete a phoneme from a word, insert a new one, and put the word back together is very difficult without well-developed literacy skills.

Most children develop phonemic awareness easily and naturally just from living in a world of language. In fact, about 80% of children develop phonemic awareness without

Table 5.1
Development of Phonological Awareness Skills

Phonological Awareness Skill	Sample Task	Relation to Reading
Recognition of rhyme and alliteration	Which words start the same? *car*, *cat*, *lock* Which word doesn't belong? *pin*, *tip*, *fin*	The ability to focus on which elements of sound make words sound the same or different is an important precursor to reading.
Phoneme blending and segmenting	What word do you get when you blend together /m/.../a/.../p/? How many sounds do you hear in *sit*?	The abilities to blend and segment the sounds in words are likely to develop along with reading ability; each supports the development of the other.
Syllable splitting and phoneme manipulation	How many sounds do you hear in the word *tent*? What word do you have when you replace the *a* in *pat* with an *i*?	These advanced skills probably develop as a result of learning to read because they are difficult without well-developed spelling skills.

any explicit instruction at all (IRA/NAEYC, 1998). Many traditional home and school activities such as reading books, reciting rhymes, and singing songs help to develop phonemic awareness by drawing children's attention to the sounds of language in the world around them.

Phonemic awareness can be integrated into every component of the kindergarten literacy program. Any time students engage in invented spelling, they are applying phonemic awareness. During shared reading, students can clap syllables and be listening detectives to hear words that rhyme or start the same way. Shared and independent writing experiences enable teachers to model and practice stretching out words and connecting words with similar sounds. Even the read-aloud affords opportunities to listen for rhythm and rhyme. Books like the Miss Bindergarten's Kindergarten series by Joseph Slate engage listeners with rhyming names. We can take advantage of opportunities to reinforce similarities and differences in sounds in almost any read-aloud, for example, the words *bears* and *Blairs* from the book *Somebody and the Three Blairs* by Marilyn Tolhurst. Some students, however, will require additional intervention in phonemic and phonological awareness, either as a result of learning difficulties or a lack of experience with language and print. For these

Adams, Foorman, Lundberg, and Beeler (1998) attest that "research clearly shows that phonemic awareness can be developed through instruction, and...doing so significantly accelerates reading and writing achievement" (p. 3). However, it is important that this instruction be just one part of the overall literacy program and embedded into other literacy experiences.

children, identification and manipulation of sounds must be made explicit and practiced in ways that are both purposeful and playful. The following activities may be helpful for developing students' phonological awareness.

Songs and Games That Play With Words and Sounds

Songs and games that emphasize rhyming and word structure can reinforce phonemic awareness in a playful way. Try tongue twisters or riddles with rhyming answers, such as "What do cats wear to keep their paws warm?" (Answer: kitten mittens!) Sing songs that manipulate the sounds in words, such as "Willowby, wallaby, wennifer, an elephant sat on Jennifer."

Elkonin Boxes

Developed by Daniel Elkonin, a Russian psychologist, the Elkonin box teaches children to manipulate phonemes by sliding a marker for every sound that they hear into a row of boxes drawn on a page. Clay (1993) found that students who have used Elkonin boxes are better able to hear sounds in words, segment words, sequence sounds, and connect sounds to letters.

Train Sounds

Helping students understand the concepts of beginning and ending sounds can be challenging for teachers. Capitalizing on many students' interest in trains, I've found it helpful to use magnetic train cars to reinforce beginning sounds (engines), medial sounds (boxcars), and ending sounds (cabooses). Trains cars can provide a powerful analogy for practicing segmenting and blending as well; students can physically separate the cars or couple (to use railroad jargon) them together as they say the sounds in various words (see Figure 5.2).

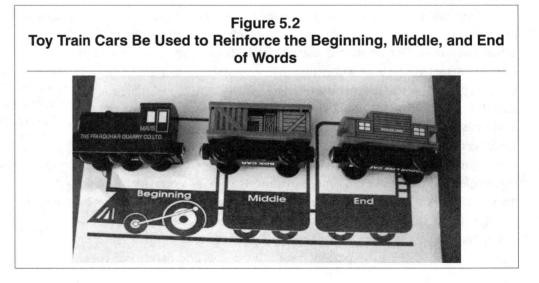

Figure 5.2
Toy Train Cars Be Used to Reinforce the Beginning, Middle, and End of Words

Sound Sorting

Sorting activities help reinforce identifying the sounds in words. Provide a collection of small objects or picture cards for students to sort by initial sound, final sound, syllables, or rhymes. (Cherry Carl has assembled several picture collections for sorting that may be downloaded from www.carlscorner.us.com/Sorts.htm.)

Invented Spelling

The NRP (NICHD, 2000) reported that, even though phonemic awareness is an oral-language skill, it is most effectively taught in conjunction with letters and sounds. Teaching students to stretch out words to hear all the sounds and to represent each sound with a letter helps reinforce both phonemic awareness and phonics. For more information, see Bubble Gum Writing in Chapter 11.

Vocabulary Development

Educators know that a strong vocabulary base has been significantly correlated with success in learning to read (NICHD, 2000). Most children learn about 600 root words per year from infancy throughout elementary school (Biemiller, 2009). But research shows that impoverished children enter school with much less vocabulary than their more economically advantaged peers (Hart & Risley, 1995). Even assuming that all students make similar progress in vocabulary development once they enter school, by grade 5, the lowest achieving students have reached only the level of an average second-grader (Biemiller, 2009). Andrew Biemiller suggests that vocabulary deficits present by grade 2 may account for differences throughout students' entire school careers. While it's important for all students to receive vocabulary instruction in early years, it's imperative for students at risk to have this instruction if they are to have success in reading and writing.

Michael Graves (2009) has identified four key elements of a strong vocabulary program: (1) providing rich and varied language experiences through listening to stories, having opportunities for speech, and receiving instruction in content areas; (2) providing explicit teaching of individual words; (3) teaching word-learning strategies; and (4) fostering awareness of and interest in words.

Explicit Teaching of Individual Words

There is no formula for determining what words should be learned in kindergarten. Beck and her colleagues (2002) define three layers of vocabulary: Tier 1 words are basic core vocabulary such as *table*, *said*, or *finger*. Tier 2 words are what we might consider "book language," which include the richer names for basic concepts, such as *crimson*, *strolled*, or *exclaimed*. Tier 3 words are technical vocabulary that usually has a very specific context, such as *evaporation*, *ecosystem*, or *multiplication*. Although Beck and her colleagues recommend that vocabulary words be chosen from Tier 2; however, many kindergarten students, like the one quoted in this chapter's title, probably need explicit instruction in Tier 1 words as well.

Books are the best tools teachers have for teaching vocabulary. Exposing kindergartners to a print-rich environment with many opportunities for shared reading and read-alouds helps them establish a foundation for strong vocabulary and other oral-language skills. Teachers frequently define or explain challenging words as they read and do their best to link the words to students' background knowledge. However, many researchers agree that these actions may not be enough (Beck et al., 2002; Biemiller, 2009; Juel, Biancarosa, Coker, & Deffes, 2003). Many students need more direct and substantial ("robust," to use Beck's word) vocabulary instruction in the early primary grades. The read-aloud is an excellent starting point for vocabulary instruction, but to make a word their own students must understand how it sounds, how it looks, how it is used, and what it means. Words need to be presented multiple times and in a variety different contexts, and the learner must be actively involved in processing the words (Beck et al., 2002).

> A typical children's story book has more unique vocabulary than an average prime time television program!
>
> *(Hayes & Ahrens, 1988)*

Research-Based Models of Vocabulary Instruction

Most vocabulary strategies for young children involve harvesting words from pictures or books. In Calhoun's (1999) Picture-Word Inductive Model, students "shake out" a collection of words from a picture, and the teacher records the words directly on the picture. This collection of words is used for practice with phonemic awareness, letter recognition, and letter-sound relations. Each student is given a collection of the words on cards to manipulate and sort based on semantics and phonetic elements, and these words are then used for guided and independent writing.

> A website created by Reading First Educators in Utah provides a wealth of Text Talk lesson plans from over 100 familiar picture books: www.schools.utah.gov/curr/readingfirst/documents/CombinedTextTalkLessons.pdf.

Beck and her colleagues' (2002) Text Talk is an analytic approach to vocabulary instruction, using vocabulary words from trade book read-alouds. A small number of key vocabulary words are selected for each story, based on the extent to which they are likely to be unfamiliar but potentially usable by young children. (A good guideline for selecting words is whether they can be clearly defined using words and concepts that are understandable to the students.) Students receive multiple exposures to each word, first in the context of the reading, then in a child-friendly definition, and then in various extended experiences with the word.

Juel and her colleagues (2003) report that analytic approaches such as Text Talk can be made richer by adding a phonetic component. This approach, called *anchored word instruction,* invites students to view the word and its component parts, to identify letter-sound relations, and to make connections between the target word and other words with similar phonetic elements.

Teach Three Words is my adaptation of these two models. It involves pulling three vocabulary words from a read-aloud to teach and reinforce. Choosing only three words from the text is the first challenge. Beck and colleagues' criteria are simple: Choose words that the students are unlikely to know yet are likely to find interesting and usable, and for which you will be able to provide child-friendly definitions. Then provide the students with a range of experiences with the word, such as the following example with the word *tiptoe*:

An example of the Teach Three Words strategy with the read-aloud *Scaredy Squirrel Makes a Friend* may be found in Chapter 6.

1. Review the word in the context of the reading. *(Remember how somebody "tiptoed" into the house?)*

2. Offer a child-friendly definition of the word. Using the word *you* in the definition helps students make a connection with the word. *(When you tiptoe, you walk on the tips of your toes, often because you want to be quiet.)*

3. Provide another example or new context for the word, unrelated to the reading. *(I might tiptoe through the wet grass so I don't get my feet wet.)*

4. Display the word on a card. Have children say the word together and note its print features. *(What do you notice about* tiptoe? *It has two little words, it has two* t*s, it has three consonants and three vowels, and it has a silent* e.*)*

5. Have students engage with the word and find other examples of it. *(If you were walking past a baby who was sleeping, would you tiptoe or not? Stand on your tiptoes for yes and on your flat feet for no. If you were marching in a band, would you tiptoe or not? Tell a partner about a time when you might tiptoe.)*

6. Post the word card on the wall, and make a tally mark any time anyone uses, sees, or hears the word in the classroom.

A Week of Wonderful Word Warm-ups

Vocabulary, phonological awareness, and oral-language forms and functions are too important to be left to chance. They affect not just school reading and writing but also students' communication skills throughout life. In a school where I was consulting, the teachers wanted to incorporate an oral-language component into their morning meeting. Together, we came up with the Week of Wonderful Word Warm-ups. Each day includes a brief (5- to 10-minute) routine that incorporates phonological awareness, word awareness, or partner talk.

A Week of Wonderful Word Warm-ups
• Mystery Monday
• Talking Tuesday
• Wow Words Wednesday
• Thinking Thursday
• Funny Friday

• **Mystery Monday** involves some sort of guessing game. It might be the mystery bags described on page 50, a cloze-style morning message for which students guess the missing words, or a Wheel of Fortune-type game for which the students guess words from given letters.

• **Talking Tuesday** focuses on extended partner talk, usually with an open-ended prompt. "Would you rather…" prompts often generate good dialogue: *Would you rather be bitten by a mosquito or stung by a bee? Would you rather eat chocolate-covered potatoes or gravy on ice cream?*

- **Wow Words Wednesday** is a vocabulary day, during which students might engage with interesting words from a shared reading text or learn "spicy synonyms" for common words such as *walked* or *said*. They might also work on partner words such as homonyms, opposites, or compounds.

- **Thinking Thursday** requires students to brainstorm, categorize, analyze, or reason in some way. They might have to generate words for a category such as "things that have buttons" or group words in a list by common attributes.

- **Funny Friday** usually involves playing with words and sounds in entertaining ways. This is a good time to incorporate phoneme manipulation games and songs. (For example, sung to the tune of "Zip-a-dee-doo-dah": *Lip-a-lee-loo-lah, lip-a-lee-lay, My, oh my, what a funny day! Lip-a-lee-loo-lah, lip-a-lee-lay, Let's sing about Lori in a silly way!*)

These engaging routines are both playful and purposeful, establishing a context for a day full of rich talk and powerful learning.

CHAPTER 6

"Read It Again!": Making the Most of the Interactive Read-Aloud

The storybook read-aloud (see Figure 6.1) has been a mainstay in kindergarten classrooms for as long as there have been kindergarten classrooms. We as teachers read aloud to kindergartners for many different reasons: to enable students to hear the fluency and flow of language and to expose them to rich vocabulary; to introduce a topic, establish a context for study, or create a quiet transition from one activity to another; to teach children about their world, provide vicarious experiences not available to them in real life, and teach them things that they didn't know before. Over a quarter century ago, the Commission on Reading asserted, "The single most important activity for building knowledge required for eventual success in reading is reading aloud to children" (Anderson, Hiebert, Scott, & Wilkinson, 1985, p. 23). That statement is every bit as true today.

**Figure 6.1
A Kindergarten Teacher Reads Aloud to Students**

Story reading, more than any other activity, provides children with information about the processes and functions of written language in a meaningful holistic context, instead of as isolated subskills. Through purposeful read-alouds, children learn to use their knowledge of the world, their knowledge of how stories work, and their personal responses to make sense of text. As Richard Robinson and Michael McKenna (2007) assert, "Research has almost universally supported the idea that reading aloud to children leads to improved reading comprehension" (p. 77).

In spite of the many merits of reading aloud, simply immersing children in books will not necessarily turn them into readers. William Teale and Junko Yokota (2000) caution that reading aloud is not a silver bullet; what children read and how they read will determine the effectiveness of the read-aloud program in nurturing children's literacy. If we want our read-aloud program to support emerging readers, we need to pay particular attention to selecting quality texts that extend students' knowledge of literature, language, and the world; we need to read, read, and reread those texts and we need to make students active participants in the reading process. That is the essence of the interactive read-aloud.

> **Three Keys to an Effective Classroom Read-Aloud:**
> 1. Selecting rich literature and nonfiction
> 2. Making students active participants in the reading process
> 3. Rereading familiar texts

There is great value in revisiting a book two, three, and even more times (IRA/NAEYC, 1998). What's the first thing students say when their teacher has finished reading aloud a great book? "Read it again!" Research consistently supports the promise of rereading texts for developing comprehension and vocabulary. Kelly Gallagher (2009) describes the first reading as "survival mode" (p. 98), during which readers are just getting control of the story. Even in kindergarten, a good story will present new insights to be gained from each reading. Rereading familiar texts also enables students to focus on language, story structure, visuals, and text features. Children comprehend and respond more deeply to books that have been read previously (Morrow, 1988). Miriam Martinez and Nancy Roser (1985) found that not only did children make more comments and connections during rereadings of familiar texts, the responses were more rich, varied, and complex. Rereading benefits all children but appears to be particularly important for children at risk (Morrow, O'Connor, & Smith, 1990).

> "Rereading both reacquaints and reassures, as well as reopens new discoveries and understandings."
>
> *(Martinez, Roser, & Dooley, 2003, p. 231)*

Selecting Books for a Read-Aloud Program

Given the sheer quantity of excellent children's books published today, perhaps the biggest challenge for teachers is choosing what books to read. The interactive read-aloud is not the place for simple, predictable, repetitive texts that lend little to growth in vocabulary, background knowledge, or comprehension. McGee and Schickedanz (2007) recommend choosing stories that contain rich vocabulary and encourage readers to make inferences about characters and plot development. When choosing fiction for young children, consider the following criteria:

- Topics that children can relate to but that extend them as learners. Familiar situations with an unusual twist enable readers to connect existing knowledge to new ideas.

- Characters that are clearly defined and few in number, preferably one main character with whom children can identify. Young readers generally prefer characters (whether human or animal) that think, act, and talk like children.

- Fast-moving plots that are logically sequenced, with a realistic problem and a satisfying resolution

- A theme or message that is subtle but appropriate to the world of a four- to six-year old

- Text that extends the children's range of vocabulary and language sense

- Illustrations that not only enhance the text but enrich it

Children need to see their own lives reflected in the books they read. In our increasingly diverse society, it's more important than ever to fill students' literate worlds with books that reflect different cultures and lifestyles. We need to honor the lives of all our students and teach them to appreciate both the differences and the similarities of the lives of those around them. In selecting multicultural literature, look for books that are accurate and authentic and that avoid stereotypes in either text or illustrations. Some examples for kindergarten include *My Two Grandmothers* by Effin Older in which a family blends Jewish and Christian traditions; *Too Many Tamales* by Gary Soto, which takes place during a South American family celebration; and nonfiction titles such as *Birthdays! Celebrating Life Around the World* by Eve Feldman or *Hello! Good-bye!* by Aliki, which teaches greetings in a variety of languages.

> "Through literature, children learn to...find themselves, imagine others, value differences, search for justice."
>
> *(Langer, 1996, p. 1)*

Nonfiction Texts

Although the storybook read-aloud is very important, it's also important to expose students to a range of different genres and text forms. Nonfiction, especially informational text, builds background knowledge and answers children's questions about their world. Laura Smolkin and Carol Donovan (2003) report that interactive read-alouds of nonfiction texts can contribute significantly to comprehension development in emergent readers. And yet, as Nell Duke found in her seminal 2000 study, the use of nonfiction was rare in most primary classrooms and almost nonexistent in high-poverty classrooms.

In the past, there were simply not very many nonfiction texts appropriate for kindergarten; today, however, many beautifully crafted informational books for young children may be found on a variety of topics to match almost any classroom theme or interest. Some considerations for choosing nonfiction read-alouds include the following:

- Current and factually accurate information

- Illustrations, especially photographs, that accurately portray the action, mood, and intent of the material
- Text with interesting and engaging style and voice

Info-text is not the only form of nonfiction that is suitable for children. Consider picture book biographies, procedural and how-to texts, and persuasive texts, such as *Should There Be Zoos: A Persuasvie Text* by Tony Stead. Nor do all read-alouds need to be in book form. Magazines, brochures, and even newspapers may be sources of nonfiction reading. However, be cautious about texts that combine fiction and nonfiction, such as The Magic School Bus series by Joanna Cole and Bruce Degen or *Diary of a Worm* and other similar titles by Doreen Cronin. These books can be delightful read-alouds but will require more deliberate attention to help students distinguish between the facts and the story.

How to Read Aloud

Most teachers don't spend a lot of time planning read-alouds. After all, there is no *wrong* way to read aloud, is there? There are things we can do, however, to make the classroom read-aloud program even better. Careful selection of books that extend students' language skills and background knowledge is a first step, but it is through purposeful teaching that we also extend students' thinking and their understanding of what readers do.

Douglas Fisher and his colleagues (Fisher, Flood, Lapp, & Frey, 2004) examined the read-aloud practices of 25 expert teachers at all grade levels and identified the following common elements:

1. Books were carefully chosen to match both the students' interests and their developmental levels.
2. Teachers previewed the texts to prepare themselves for both the oral reading and points of discussion.
3. Each read-aloud served a clearly articulated purpose.
4. Teachers read with fluency, expression, and animation.
5. Connections were made to independent reading and writing.
6. Teachers stopped periodically and thoughtfully questioned the students to focus them on specifics of the text.

Many studies have linked talk about text to greater literacy growth (Hickman, 1981; Langer, 1996; Lehr, 1988). David Dickinson and Michael Smith (1994) found, however, that the amount of growth was related not just to general conversation about the reading but also to the amount of *analytic* talk students did—that is, talk that involved drawing inferences or relating different parts of a story. Even young children can analyze text and illustrations to construct meaning during reading (Sipe, 2000), draw inferences about themes (Lehr, 1988), and

> Literacy growth is enhanced by analytic talk about reading.

make connections to prior knowledge and experience (Cochran-Smith, 1984). Students engage more deeply with reading when they are invited to ask questions, make predictions, draw inferences, make judgments, and offer personal responses. Teaching young children to engage in analytic talk requires skillful modeling and thinking aloud as well as encouraging, prompting, scaffolding, and probing them to dig deeper into the text.

> If we wait until after reading to discuss a story, we are missing out on valuable literacy opportunities.

Effective storybook reading is an interactive process. Too often, we don't allow students to interact with text while it is being read, insisting that they wait until after the reading is done. If students are given the opportunity, however, the richest discussions often take place *during* the reading. Lawrence Sipe (2000) suggests that allowing students to talk during the story reading enables the teacher to guide and support them in constructing meaning during the reading. When the teacher precedes the reading by inviting predictions and personal connections, he or she creates a context for the reading. Taking time to discuss and clarify difficult concepts during the reading can prevent misunderstanding further on, and encouraging students to respond during the reading enhances both comprehension and interest in the story. Pausing to confirm and revise predictions, ask questions, and make inferences lays the groundwork for independent reading. In this way, students learn that making meaning from text is a process that occurs before, during, and after reading.

McGee and Schickedanz (2007) have developed an approach to the kindergarten read-aloud in which a carefully selected text is read aloud three times to develop comprehension and encourage analytic talk among students. The first reading involves a book introduction, fluent oral reading of the text, vocabulary clarification during reading, teacher modeling of analytic comments at a few strategic points, and a "big idea" question for discussion after reading. The second reading occurs no more than one or two days after the first and involves more elaborate vocabulary descriptions and more pauses for students to respond to teacher prompts and questions. The third reading takes place several days later—to encourage long-term memory—and involves a guided reconstruction of the story during which students recount information and engage in guided discussions that extend and enrich the reading experience.

> "Effective interactive read-alouds include a systematic approach that incorporates teachers' modeling of higher level thinking, asking thoughtful questions calling for analytic talk, and prompting children to recall a story in some way."
>
> *(McGee & Schickedanz, 2007, p. 11)*

Planning an Interactive Read-Aloud Sequence

Some teachers fear that making the classroom read-aloud interactive will turn it into a free-for-all in which students blurt out random comments throughout the reading and lose the thread of the story entirely. That's why it's important to carefully plan each read-aloud session to include purposeful "pause points" and prompts to model thinking and focus discussion. Rather than distracting the students, these interactions actually enhance and enrich experiences with the text because the students become active participants in constructing meaning from the reading. A sample read-aloud sequence using the book *Scaredy Squirrel Makes a Friend* by Mélanie Watt (2007) is found in Figure 6.2.

Figure 6.2
An Interactive Read-Aloud Sequence for *Scaredy Squirrel Makes a Friend* by Mélanie Watt

Book Introduction: The 3 Ps

Preview Text: *You may have heard of a "scaredy cat," but have you ever heard of a "scaredy squirrel"? Scaredy Squirrel is scared of everything. He wants to find a friend, but he doesn't want to be friends with anything that might bite him.*

Prior Knowledge: Use interactive writing to answer the question, *What are we scared of/not scared of?* (See photo of sample interactive writing.)

What makes a good friend? Who might be a good friend for a squirrel?
Purpose: *Let's read to see who Scaredy finds for a friend.*

First Reading: Read fluently and expressively, briefly explaining words or ideas as necessary for students to understand the story.

Pause Point 1: *Do you think a fish would be a perfect friend? Why or why not?*

Pause Point 2: *I wonder why Scaredy needs all those things. What do you think?*

Pause Point 3: *What do you think might happen with the dog?*

"Big Idea" Question: Discuss with a partner the question, *Which do you think would make a better friend, a fish or a dog?*

(continued)

Figure 6.2 *(continued)*
An Interactive Read-Aloud Sequence for *Scaredy Squirrel Makes a Friend* by Mélanie Watt

Second Reading: Reread the entire story, stopping more frequently for explanation and discussion, depending on the interests of the students and points of confusion. Do a collaborative retelling of the story.

Teach three words:

1. *perfect*: Scaredy is looking for a *perfect* friend.
2. *dangerous*: Scaredy was afraid that some animals might be *dangerous*.
3. *spots*: Scaredy *spots* a fish through his binoculars.

"Big Idea" Question: *What advice would you give Scaredy about being a good friend?*

Third Reading: Before reading, invite students to retell the story. Reread the story, pausing to confirm or correct elements of the retelling or as student interest or questions dictate. Focus on vocabulary and text features.

Pause Point 1: Look at the map feature and how it tells the story. Point out the various elements of the map and discuss what purpose they serve. Talk about why the author chose to put a map in this section.

Pause Point 2: Look at the labeled diagrams. What kinds of information do they provide?

Shared or Interactive Writing: Create a labeled diagram of an animal. Model how to draw arrows to different parts of its body and label the arrows with words.

Independent Response: Invite students to create their own labeled diagrams with an animal of their own choice (see example).

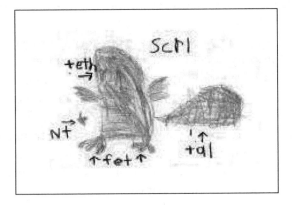

Before Reading

The first step in planning a read-aloud lesson is to choose the text and determine the purpose for reading. The nex step is to think about how you are going to introduce the book to the students. A well-crafted book introduction establishes a context, sets the tone, and helps readers activate necessary background knowledge. I like to think about the 3 Ps of a book introduction: (1) preview, (2) prior knowledge, and (3) purpose. I might *preview* the text with my students by displaying the cover, introducing the author and illustrator, and providing a brief summary of the book's contents. Sometimes I encourage my students to "picture walk" through the book to invite predictions or anticipatory discussion. Depending on the story, I might introduce the characters, setting, and the problem or plot. Activating prior knowledge opens that schema folder in the readers' minds that stores all the information that they already know about the topic. This is particularly important when reading nonfiction texts because the writer often assumes that the reader is bringing certain background knowledge to the experience.

3 Ps Book Introduction
1. Preview
2. Prior knowledge
3. Purpose for reading

Finally, I want to set a purpose for the reading. "I wonder" statements, such as "I wonder how the pigs will trick the wolf," help to provide a focus for students as they listen to the read-aloud. Sometimes the purpose will be strategy based, such as "Let's read to see if our prediction was right" or "As you listen, I want you to think about what you're wondering about the story." A purpose for reading nonfiction might be "Let's read to see which of our 'think we know' facts were confirmed in the book and what new facts we might learn." (See Figure 6.3 for more on making a What We Think We Know chart.)

During Reading

We as teachers already know the importance of reading fluently and expressively and varying tone, volume, and pitch during reading. It can be a challenge for us to read with animation while holding the book so everyone can see the illustrations, maintaining frequent eye contact with the students, and sharing our own observations and processes as a reader, all at the same time. That's why it's often necessary to prepare and practice the reading—even for a kindergarten read-aloud.

As you read, model your own responses to the story, pausing occasionally to revisit predictions, express curiosity or confusion, or comment on something you found interesting. Be sure to explain ideas or words you think students might not understand, and feel free to improvise if you think a concept needs elaboration or you must replace a word that is inappropriate.

Plan ahead of time three or four strategic pause points throughout the reading to invite students to "talk to your neighbor" (TTYN). Keep these interactions short (a minute or two) and focused by providing a prompt or question. It's not always necessary to share the dialogue with the whole group, but you will want to eavesdrop on the conversations in your classroom to assess students' thinking and comprehension. Keeping a notebook on hand to record anecdotal notes or ideas is also helpful.

Figure 6.3
What We Think We Know Chart

As a prereading tool for nonfiction, I like to use a modification of the Reading and Analyzing Nonfiction organizer developed by Tony Stead (2006). I fold a sheet of chart paper in half, like a book. The front of the book is labeled *What We Think We Know*, the two sections of the inside are labeled *We Were Right!* and *What We Learned*, and the back is labeled *What We Still Wonder*.

Before reading, I invite the students to tell anything they think they know about the topic, and I record all their ideas on sticky notes. Each sticky note is attached to the What We Think We Know section of the book. (Anyone who has had a kindergartner inform them in no uncertain terms, "Penguins can dance; I saw it on the movie" will agree that it's dangerous to treat these statements as facts!) After reading, we go back and look for What We Think We Know facts that were confirmed by what we read. These sticky notes are moved to the inside of the book under the heading We Were Right! We also record any new facts that were learned and place those sticky notes in the What We Learned section of the book.

I find that questions or "wonderings" about the topic are much more focused on the topic if we generate them *after* reading, so we record our questions on sticky notes and post them at the back of the book in the What We Still Wonder section. If students can find answers to the questions, they may write the answers on sticky notes and add them to this page as well.

In addition to activating prior knowledge, the What We Think We Know chart or "book" sets up a purpose for reading—to find out what facts are confirmed in the text and what new facts we will learn. After reading, we can use the We Were Right! and What We Learned facts for a variety of purposes, including sorting, vocabulary development, and interactive writing.

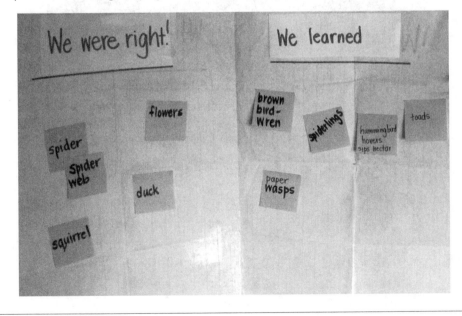

These purposeful and strategic stopping places in the reading to think-aloud, invite students to turn and talk to a partner, or both must be carefully planned to enhance the students' experience with the text and boost their comprehension while retaining the thread of the story. I often mark my books with sticky notes to remind myself of think-aloud comments I will make or questions I will ask to prompt and probe the students' thinking.

Comprehension Strategies During Read-Aloud. The kindergarten read-aloud may be the best opportunity teachers have to introduce the strategies that good readers use. I generally focus on three explicit comprehension strategies with kindergartners: (1) questioning ("I'm wondering..."), (2) connecting ("This is like…"), and (3) interpreting ("I'm thinking..."). Using gestures and props or visuals helps reinforce these processes and make them more concrete (Block, Parris, & Whiteley, 2008; Oczkus, 2004). For example, when I introduce wondering statements to a kindergarten class, I bring in a rain stick to show to the students. Without saying a word, I just start moving it back and forth to create the rain sound. Inevitably, the students start asking questions: What is that? How does it make that noise? What's inside the stick? What's it for? I tell them that just as they wondered about the stick, readers wonder about the ideas in stories. We use the wonder stick and a shrugging gesture to remind us about wondering when we read (see Figure 6.4). As I read aloud, I pause

> **Think-Aloud Prompts**
> - I wonder...
> - This reminds me of...
> - I don't understand….
> - Oh! Now I get it…
> - I'm thinking that…
> - I predict that…
> - I used to think…but now I think…

Figure 6.4
The "I Wonder" Stick Reinforces Questioning During Reading

a few times to model the gesture and share my "wonderings." Then I give the students opportunities to make the "I wonder" gesture and talk to a partner about what they are wondering. When we bring the conversation to the whole group, I let different students hold the wonder stick as they tell what they are wondering. The challenge, of course, is keeping the wonderings focused on the text, but with plenty of modeling and careful prompting, the students learn to link their thinking to the reading. The chart in Table 6.1 shows the language and gestures to use for all three strategies.

Table 6.1
Language and Gestures for Questioning, Connecting, and Interpreting

I Say	I Do	Prop
I wonder…	Shrug	Wonder stick
I connect…, This reminds me…, This is like…	Link fingers	Plastic links on a chain
I think…, I guess…, I predict…	Tap head	Flashlight

I want students to use these comprehension strategies, but, just as important, I want them to know they are using them. I use the actions during my think-alouds (which also help students distinguish between when I'm thinking aloud and when I'm reading), and I invite students to gesture during TTYN time to indicate the strategy they are talking about.

Vocabulary During Read-Aloud. The read-aloud is also the best vehicle teachers have for making deposits into students' word banks. As we read aloud, we may spontaneously explain or elaborate on unfamiliar words for the students, but the read-aloud also offers many opportunities for more systematic and explicit vocabulary instruction. Teach Three Words involves pulling three vocabulary words from the reading to teach and reinforce. Choose three words that the students are unlikely to know, words that students are likely to find interesting and usable, and words that you will be able to define for the students using words and concepts they will understand. Then provide the students with multiple experiences with the word, such as the example with the word *tiptoe* on page 57.

After Reading

In the past, many teachers have felt compelled to plan some sort of follow-up or extension to the reading. In truth, not all books lend themselves to cooking, crafts, or the Crayola curriculum. Extension activities should develop naturally from the text and extend students' literacy development and higher level thinking. What kind of discussion will follow the reading? How can this discussion enrich the students' experience with the text and make them better readers, writers, and thinkers?

Retelling is an effective tool for assessing and enhancing comprehension (Gambrell & Dromsky, 2000). It requires students to think about story structure, distinguish main ideas, and use the language of the story. However, before kindergartners can be expected to retell a story effectively, they need to be taught how to do a retell. It's important to model retelling stories; teach children the concepts of beginning, middle, and end; name and define characters; and distinguish key events. As students learn to retell, teachers can scaffold them by starting the story and inviting them to continue it as well as providing prompt if the students falter or get off track. Even prompts like, "Tell me more" or "Then what happened?" can generate more detail in the retelling. Sometimes having a visual aid or prop, such as a puppet or toy, can trigger reminders of the text or support students' retelling. Some retelling tools include the following:

- The Shape-Go Map (Benson & Cummins, 2000) consists of a triangle, a rectangle, and a circle to represent the beginning, middle, and end of a story (see Figure 6.6). Students trace around the shapes as they retell each part of the story. I like to color-code them green, yellow, and red like traffic lights. The green triangle represents the beginning of the story, and the reteller runs his or her finger along each side as he or she explains the characters, setting, and problem. The yellow rectangle represents the middle of the story and the reteller traces each side of the shape as he or she relates at least four key events. Finally, the red circle represents the ending, which circles around to the beginning by explaining how the problem was solved and how the story ends.

- Props such as a purple plastic purse (for *Lily's Purple Plastic Purse* by Kevin Henkes) or an owl puppet (for *Owl Moon* by Jane Yolen) engage students with the story and can be helpful reminders to motivate a retelling.

- Spinners, dice, or word cards invite students at random to tell certain parts of the story. Each section or card contains a prompt, such as those found in the box to the left.

- To make a Retelling Ribbon string several beads on a piece of ribbon for students to touch as they retell each part of the story. The beads might be color-coded, such as using a purple bead for characters, yellow for the setting, green for the problem or initiating event, three or four blue beads for

---

Create retelling dice, cards, or spinners with prompts such as the following:

- Tell something about one of the characters.
- Tell something about where the story took place.
- Tell something about the problem and how it was solved.
- Tell something about how the story ended.
- Tell about your favourite part of the story.
- Tell about one part of the story you would change if you were the author.

When retelling a story, teach students to tell these things:

- Who the main characters are
- Where and when the story took place
- What important event or problem started the story
- What important things happened in the story
- How the story ended

key events in the story, a red bead for the conclusion, and a black bead for a response or connection.

Shared and interactive writing experiences are other ways to have students respond to a read-aloud. Topics or themes from the read-aloud may be springboards for new writing pieces, or "text innovations" may be created based on a pattern or structure in the book. Figure 6.2 on pages 64–65 shows student writing using the technique of labeled diagrams after reading *Scaredy Squirrel Makes a Friend*.

Always make the book available to students after a read-aloud. The books that are read aloud in class are the books students are most likely to choose for independent reading (Martinez & Teale, 1988). Imaginative play and creative drama will emerge naturally from reading experiences, especially when prompted by a copy of the book and a collection of props in the reading corner. For example, a black pot, some spaghetti made from pieces of yarn, a scarf, and a broom may be all children need to extend their experience with *Strega Nona* by Tomi dePaola). Jodi Welsch (2008) found that when her students were provided with some simple costumes and props, they engaged in both "play within text," which consisted of close reenactments of the stories, and "play beyond text," which involved adding some element of character, plot, or dialogue to the story.

Figure 6.6
A Shape-Go Map Guides Students in Retelling the Beginning, Middle, and End of a Story

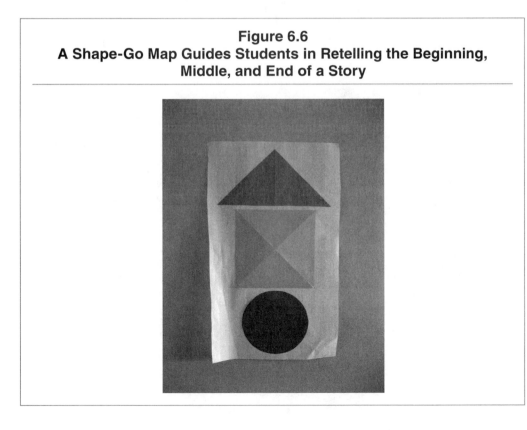

Reading aloud can be an important way to develop skilled and engaged readers because students learn about the language of books and the structure of story through listening to read-alouds. They gain access to new and complex concepts, creating background knowledge on which to build further learning. Through sensitive scaffolding of students' questions and conversations, we can bridge even the youngest students to higher levels of thinking, communicating, and responding to text.

CHAPTER 7

"All Together Now!": Shared Reading With Big Books, Poems, and Posters

It seems that some children learn to read almost magically, just by being read to. Yet Durkin's (1966) classic research showed that most children who came to school reading had been the beneficiaries of much incidental instruction from parents. When parents and children cuddle together to read a book, they usually talk about the story and pictures. They share their reactions and recite familiar passages together. They may even point out letters and words. These interactions with text create a solid foundation for learning to read.

Unfortunately, even the most generous lap can't hold 20 or more students. So how can we teachers replicate the benefits of the bedtime story in a school setting? Over 30 years ago, Don Holdaway (1979) and his colleagues in New Zealand created what they called the "shared book experience" (p. 129). By enlarging text to make it visible to groups of children, they were able to model the reading process and, at the same time, draw children's attention to concepts of print and letter knowledge that they would not otherwise notice from simply listening to a story read aloud. The shared reading experience is intended, first and foremost, to expose children to the joy of reading and entice them to want to be readers themselves. However, shared reading also provides students with systematic and explicit instruction in negotiating print and understanding text features. This is what distinguishes shared reading from the traditional read-aloud.

Shared reading takes many forms in the kindergarten classroom, including Big Books, language experience charts, and print projected on a screen. Regardless of the medium, there are certain common elements to the shared book experience:

- Enlarged print and illustrations accessible to all
- Modeling of reading by a teacher or more experienced reader
- Repeated readings for comprehension, fluency, and focus on print features

Shared reading experiences benefit kindergartners by helping them do the following:

- Take pleasure in reading
- Engage with reading materials that are too difficult for them to read independently
- Develop concepts of print and phonological awareness
- Build phonetic skills in the context of connected text
- Learn to use meaning, structure, and visual cues to monitor and self-correct
- Identify high-frequency words
- Build comprehension strategies such as predicting and connecting to prior knowledge
- Learn to identify and understand text features and story text structures
- Think, act, and see themselves as readers

Changing voices adds a level of novelty to rereading familiar text and build fluency and expression. Some favorite "voices" include the following:

• Squeaky mouse

• Giant (deep)

• Underwater (with plugged noses)

• Opera singer

• Cowboy

• Turtle (very slow)

During a shared reading lesson, students observe and gradually participate through multiple readings of a text (see Figure 7.1). The first reading usually focuses on understanding and appreciating the story as the teacher models fluent and expressive oral reading, sometimes thinking aloud about his or her reading processes or responses to the text. Subsequent readings are used to draw students' attention to the print and how it works. The teacher uses techniques such as tracking the print, pointing out spaces between words, or highlighting graphophonic elements such as initial sounds or letter patterns. The text is read several more times, with students gradually chiming in with the teacher as they become comfortable and familiar with the text.

Shared reading lessons are designed to be fast paced, interactive, and multilevel. One of the most powerful aspects of the shared reading structure is that every student can take something unique from the experience, depending on his or her stage of development and level of engagement.

Figure 7.1
Shared Reading Enables Groups of Students to Participate in the Reading Process

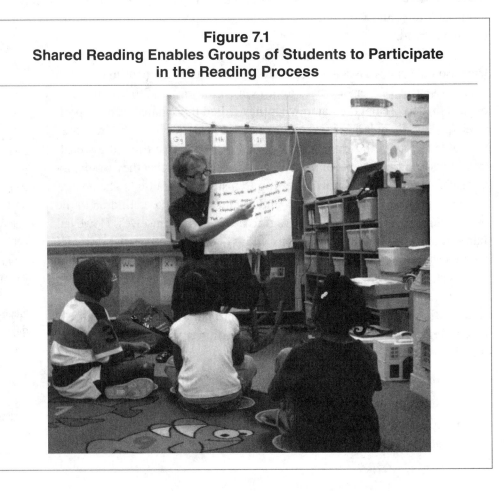

Choosing Texts for Shared Reading

Experience charts, pocket charts, and posters are the traditional media for shared reading, but today's technology has opened new doors for access to texts. Interactive whiteboards, document projectors, and even the lowly overhead projector can be used to enlarge a piece of text. Not just any piece of enlarged text will be effective for shared reading, however.

When Holdaway (1979) and his colleagues first developed the shared book experience, they focused mainly on enlarging traditional tales such as "The Three Billy Goats Gruff" and "The Gingerbread Man" for their simple story lines, rhythmical and repetitious language, and dramatic endings. Still, these stories were rich enough to be revisited over and over for added layers of understanding.

Today, there are a multitude of Big Books and other enlarged print resources available to us, but not all work well for shared reading. While we want the shared reading experience to stretch students as readers, most of the stories we select as read-alouds have too much print on the page and are too complicated for shared book experiences. For example, it's easy to find Big Book versions of such familiar titles as *Chrysanthemum* by Kevin Henkes and *The Paper Bag Princess* by Robert Munsch. Although they are delightful read-alouds, these texts are simply not suited for shared reading because of the challenging vocabulary and amount of print on the page. Young readers are unlikely to be able to join in the reading, no matter how many times the text is revisited. When choosing commercial Big Books for shared reading in kindergarten, look for books with simple, repetitive language, just a few lines of text on each page, and illustrations that closely match the text.

The same guidelines for text selection that Holdaway followed 30 years ago remain useful today. Consider the three Rs of shared reading: (1) rhythm, (2) repetition, and (3) rhyme. Brenda Parkes (2000), the author of many books written especially for shared reading, recommends the following considerations:

- Clear, readable print with ample space between words and lines
- Rich, memorable language
- A strong, satisfying story line with a predictable structure
- Bright, vigorous illustrations that support the text

Published Big Books are often costly, but the classroom library can be supplemented with class-made and teacher-made oversize books. Traditional rhymes, chants, and songs make excellent charts or illustrated books. You can word-process the text, enlarging the font to a readable size (at least 24 points), and add clip art or student illustrations.

> "The books must delight the children and be worth returning to again and again."
>
> *(Parkes, 2000, p. 117)*

Shared Reading With Big Books

Big Books are often trade books printed in enlarged format, although some are created specifically to be Big Books. Shared reading of Big Books enables the teacher to model and demonstrate reading processes using full-length stories and nonfiction texts.

The shared book experience begins much like the interactive read-aloud. It should start with a 3 Ps book introduction: (1) preview the text, (2) activate prior knowledge, and (3) set a purpose for reading. The book preview might be as simple as a one-sentence overview of the main idea or as elaborate as a picture walk through the entire book. Often, in my classes we play the Show What You Know game. I'll display the cover of the book to the students without reading the title and invite individuals to come up and point out pictures, letters, and words that they recognize. Everyone wins: the student who knows only the pictures, the student who can identify a letter or two, and the student who can read whole words or the entire title.

> The Show What You Know game invites students to point out elements of print and pictures that they recognize from the cover of the book, honoring what each child brings to the reading experience.

During the first reading of the book, the teacher reads aloud, pausing occasionally to comment or reflect. He or she stops at a couple of predetermined pause points for students to turn and talk to a partner about a specific question or strategy (such as "What are you wondering right now?" or "What do you predict is going to happen next?"). This initial exposure to the text focuses on comprehension and enjoyment of the story or information.

> Establish predetermined pause points during which students are invited to turn and talk with a partner about what they are thinking or wondering.

On subsequent readings, the teacher might delve deeper into the text; however, because shared reading texts are less complex than texts for read-aloud, they are less likely to have multiple layers of meaning. As the students become more familiar with the text, they join in on reading familiar parts, especially those that are repeated. This activity builds fluency by encouraging students to read chorally and connect what they see on the page to what they say and hear. The teacher might also include a vocabulary focus, such as Teach Three Words, described in Chapters 5 and 6.

What shared reading lends itself to most effectively, however, is focusing on letter and word studies in the context of connected text. There are a number of playful and purposeful activities that students can engage in to attend to text:

- Hunt for specific letters, words, and text features.
- Cover a word with a sticky note and have others guess the word.
- Highlight specific words or letters with removable highlighting tape.
- Underline or circle words or letters with waxed string.

It's not necessary to spend a lot of money on reading manipulatives. Many inexpensive items for tracking or framing print may be found at your local dollar store (see Figure 7.2).

Reading manipulatives like those in the following list add fun, variety, and interest to word study. They make each reading a new adventure. Nothing compares to the empowerment kindergartners feel when they can actually read a text!

After reading, the teacher may retell the story or engage students in an interactive writing experience. Interactive or shared writing activities often involve creating a new piece of writing based on the theme, pattern, or text features of the book used for shared

---

Figure 7.2
Reading Manipulatives From the Dollar Store

Each rereading is a new experience when we use different pointers and framers each time.

- Anything with a point may be used for tracking: magic wands, cocktail swizzle sticks, chopsticks, pointers, bubble wands.
- Anything with a hole may be used for framing words: tracing toys; magnifying glasses or fly swatters with holes cut in the center; the center of plastic letters, such as *O* or *D*; toy bracelets or rings.
- The lenses can be removed from sunglasses to create special reading glasses.

---

reading. For example, a class might create books like "Children, Children, What Do You See?" (based on *Brown Bear, Brown Bear* by Bill Martin Jr) or "Harry the Hamster's Week" (based on *Cookie's Week* by Cindy Ward). Other shared or interactive writing experiences from shared reading might include the following:

- Summarizing or retelling what happened in the text
- Writing a letter to or from a character
- Creating another story with the character in the book
- Writing "all about" books on a topic related to the book
- Recreating part of the story in a different form such as "how-to"

The final step in the shared reading experience is to place the book in the reading corner for students to access on their own. Martinez and Teale (1988) found that, of all the books in the classroom library, students are most likely to try to read conventionally the Big Books that have been read in class.

Shared Reading With a Poem of the Week

Using short poems for shared reading affords many of the same learning opportunities as Big Books. Following is a sample poem-of-the-week cycle with a different focus for each day:

Day 1: Echo reading

1. Introduce the poem. Read it aloud, modeling fluency and expression.
2. Read the poem a second time, having students echo you after each line.
3. Talk about the ideas in the poem. Invite personal connections, wonderings, and responses.

4. Invite students to join in as you read the poem again. In subsequent readings, as students' voices get stronger, gradually fade your voice and let them take over.

Day 2: Text matching

1. Read the whole poem again, inviting students to join in and fading your own voice when appropriate. Track each word with your finger as you read. Have students take turns reading in different ways such as divided into groups of boys and girls or reading with funny voices.

2. Provide an additional copy of individual words, phrases, and lines for students to match to the poem.

Day 3: Work with the words

1. Reread the poem, with students leading the tracking. Let the leader choose the tracking tool.

2. Invite students to frame individual words with their hands.

3. Identify rhymes or high-frequency words that students already know. This is a wonderful opportunity to harvest words for the high-frequency word wall.

4. Cover some of the words with blank cards or sticky notes, and have students guess the words. Uncover one letter at a time to invite their predictions. Write the hidden words on index cards, and have students identify the words that go into the blanks.

5. Write words on sticky notes and substitute them for words in the text. Have students identify and replace the incorrect words.

Day 4: Work with letters and sounds

1. Choose word features to highlight—rhyming words, twin letters, action words. Have students use highlighting tape, or waxed string to point out these words (see Figure 7.3).

2. Practice blending and segmenting specific words, using Elkonin boxes (described in Chapter 5).

3. Make lists of words from the text and sort them (e.g., by syllables, beginning or ending sound, vowel sound, or meaning).

4. Have students brainstorm other words that go with words or patterns from the poem.

Day 5: Individual poems

1. Give each student his or her own copy of the poem for individual poetry books.

2. Have students read and highlight specific text features.

3. Invite students to illustrate their poems and add them to their book boxes for independent reading.

Figure 7.3
Highlighting Tape May Be Used to Focus on Words or Letters in Text

Shared Reading With Pocket Chart Texts

The pocket chart is a particularly useful literacy tool for reading and manipulating lines, phrases, and words in text. Often traditional nursery rhymes or contemporary short poems (preferably four to eight lines) are used for pocket chart reading. Each line of the text is written on a sentence strip and placed in the clear plastic pockets.

Terry Johnson and Daphne Louis (1987) suggest the following sequence of shared language activities using pocket charts: recognizing, identifying, matching, sorting, and finally manipulating text. Start with the whole poem, then go through each step with individual lines of text. Only when the students are familiar with lines do you go back into the poem to work with phrases, and finally words, always returning to the whole text at the beginning and end of each segment. Figure 7.4 provides a suggested pocket chart routine.

> Keep tools such as scissors, markers, highlighting tape, sticky notes, and extra sentence strips tucked into the pocket chart at all times, so you don't have to interrupt a lesson to get supplies.

Shared Reading Using Language Experience Charts

Language experience charts enable students to see their speech written down. As described in Chapter 10, students generate ideas that the teacher records; this is also

Figure 7.4
A Suggested Routine for Pocket Chart Reading

1. *Recognizing text:* After reading the whole text several times, draw attention to individual lines. Read each line, framing it as you read, then ask, "What does this line say?" Invite students to respond, then have the whole class read the line together.

2. *Identifying text:* Read the text, framing each line as you read, then ask, "Where does it say...?" Students must respond by framing the appropriate line.

3. *Matching text:* Prepare a second set of sentence strips for the pocket chart text. Display the complete rhyme in the pocket chart or tack it to the wall. Beside it, arrange the second set of sentence strips in random order. Ask students to read the first line in the poem and find the sentence strip that matches it. When a strip is identified, hold it directly under the other line for students to determine whether it matches. If there is an incorrect match, ask a student to explain why it is does not match.

4. *Sorting and sequencing text (mix and fix):* When students are thoroughly familiar with the poem, put the strips in the pocket chart in random order and have students sequence them. Invite students to mix up the lines and see if the group can read the resulting silly poem. This is an opportunity to assess whether students are reciting the poem from memory or actually beginning to access the print.

5. *Manipulating text (modified cloze):* Use scissors to cut up the lines of text and remove individual words, one at a time, from the whole text for students to identify. Leaving the rest of the line intact, turn the word card face down, or replace it with a blank card as a word marker. When the missing word is guessed or identified, return it to its place. Start by removing only a few words, and each time the routine is repeated, remove more cards. When choosing which words to remove, always start with concrete nouns first, then action verbs, and finally modifiers. Structure words such as prepositions, pronouns, articles, and auxiliary verbs are the most difficult to identify in isolation.
   Some variations of modified cloze include the following:

   • Having the missing word cards displayed for students to find and replace

   • Giving the word cards to individual students as they are removed, and as the text is read, each child replaces his or her word

   • Removing all but structure words and having the children rebuild the rhyme word by word and reread the rhyme frequently as it is built

   • Substituting words that do not make sense (such as *"Jack and Jill went up the street"*) and inviting students to identify the incorrect word and find the correct word

referred to as *shared writing*. While the teacher writes, he or she explains the process of transcribing spoken words into print, such as stretching out words, using spacing between words, and adding capital letters and punctuation. Experience charts may serve a range of topics and purposes such as sharing class news, presenting a reader's response to a text, or recording the changes in the classroom amaryllis plant as it grows.

Experience charts are a wonderful medium for shared reading activities, as they enable students to read their own words in print. Because this writing is connected to objects or events in their lives, emergent readers will have an easier time reading it and will often copy words from it when writing independently. We can revisit the charts over and over, focusing on different aspects of graphophonics and print features.

After creating an experience chart with the class, you may want to assemble it into a class Big Book. The chart can be cut into individual lines, and each student gets his or her own line. (Some children may be given the opportunity to cut their lines into individual words and then reassemble them like a jigsaw puzzle.) Students can glue their lines to large pieces of paper and add illustrations. These pages may be laminated and coil bound for durability into a class Big Book, which is guaranteed to be a popular item in the classroom library.

> Play I Spy games with experience charts.
> I spy with my little eye…
> • a word that starts the same as David
> • a word that has twin letters
> • a word that has an *s*
> • a word with three syllables
> • a word that rhymes with ball
> • a word that starts with an uppercase letter

Shared Reading Using Interactive Charts

Interactive charts enable students to physically manipulate elements of text. Elements of text that can be manipulated may include entire lines and phrases, or individual words such as rhymes, names, concrete nouns, number words, or active verbs. Interactive charts are created by preparing a rhyme, song, or finger play in enlarged text and providing a means by which certain chunks of text may be removed or replaced by another chunk of text. For example, in the nursery rhyme "Jack be nimble, Jack be quick, Jack jump over the candlestick," the name can be changed each time: "Kyle be nimble, Kyle be quick…" In a song like "Old McDonald Had a Farm," students may substitute different animals and their corresponding sounds. This substitution can lead to many opportunities for developing phonological awareness, such as counting syllables, rhyming words, or matching initial sounds. Figure 7.5 provides a sample activity with a short rhyme called "Popcorn, popcorn."

There are several ways that a chart can be adapted to facilitate manipulation:

- Attach paper fasteners to the chart so word cards can be hole punched and hung in place.

- Use a small piece of Velcro, magnetic tape, or sticky tack on both the chart and the word cards.

- Create a transparent pocket using a piece of acetate taped over the word(s) to be substituted.

Figure 7.5
Sample Interactive Chart Activity

Write this rhyme on sentence strips:
Popcorn, Popcorn, Yum, yum, yum,
Don't you wish that you had some?

Glue the strips to a large chart or board. Use sentence strips with contrasting colors on the background paper to help students see where the lines begin and end.

Read or sing the text (depending on the text and your talent), tracking each word with your finger or a pointer. Take time to reread and enjoy the whole text many times before drawing attention to specific text elements. Do not introduce a manipulation until students are totally familiar with the text as a whole. On another day, revisit the text to introduce the interactive component. Have some replacement words, such as *pizza, cookies,* or *chocolate* already prepared. Substitute the new words and read the rhyme together each time. Invite individual students to track the words as they are read.

Invite students to offer ideas for replacement words. Write their suggestions on word cards, and read the text with the new ideas in place. Clap out syllables in the words (e.g., *pop-corn, rice, pep-per-o-ni, cha-pa-ti*).

Have the chart and manipulatives available for students to work with during independent reading or center time.

Participating in shared reading activities can have a powerful impact on children's literacy development. Dickinson (1989) found that a shared reading program "dramatically increased children's engagement with books and print in particular" (p. 229), helping them construct knowledge about print and develop self-confidence as readers. However, he cautioned that the type of text, pace of lessons, and focus on textual features inherent in a shared reading experience usually create limited opportunities for extended dialogue about the story and do little to develop higher level thinking (Dickinson & Smith, 1994). Therefore, it is important that the shared book experience be just one part of an overall balanced literacy program that provides many opportunities for reading by, with, and to students to nurture all aspects of their literacy development.

CHAPTER 8

"Now I Use My Strategies": Small-Group Reading Instruction in Kindergarten

Henry was excited to read his little book to me when I visited his classroom. I signed my "autograph" on the sticky note in the back of his book to indicate that he had read to me, then commented, "Wow, have you always been such a good reader?" "No, I didn't use to be that good," he replied seriously, "but now I use my strategies and I can read anything I want!"

I confess that I haven't always been very comfortable with the idea of guided reading in kindergarten. After all, if you consider guided reading to be a process of scaffolding readers as they make meaning from print, it's pretty difficult when students are not yet negotiating print! However, when I came to accept that guided reading looked a little different in kindergarten than at any other stage of development, I realized that there was much to be gained by working with groups of students like Henry to develop the skills and strategies they need to become successful readers.

We as teachers pull individual students and groups aside for instruction for many purposes in kindergarten. We might work with one group on reading and retelling an emergent-level text and another group to work on beginning and ending sounds in words. I view both as guided reading in kindergarten. We choose a particular text for its level of challenge and support for the students in the group and use that text for both comprehension and word study.

Marcia Kosanovich and her colleagues (2006) distinguish between two alternative small-group structures: (1) guided reading involves supporting students as they flexibly apply a range of strategies to processing text at graduated levels of difficulty, and (2) skills-focused lessons address one or more specific areas of need for a particular group of students. I argue that the two structures don't need to be mutually exclusive. Some teachers believe that guided reading focuses only on comprehension, while skills lessons focus on word solving. I think guided reading should do both. Purists may protest, but in this chapter I use the terms *guided reading* and *small-group reading* interchangeably.

Here's how I see guided reading (see Figure 8.1): It's a learning structure that focuses on small, flexible, needs-based groups that are regularly

Elements of Guided Reading:

- Small, needs-based groups that are changed frequently as needed.
- Texts that are carefully selected for their level of difficulty as well as their support for specific focus strategies and skills.
- Teacher support and guidance as students practice the focus skills with connected text.

Figure 8.1
Guided Reading Enables Emergent Readers to Access Print Individually and With Teacher Support

changed to meet students' needs. It uses texts that have been carefully selected not just for their reading levels but also because they lend themselves to specific focus skills and strategies. It provides students with opportunities to practice both text-level (comprehension) and word-level strategies in the context of connected reading and with teacher support. The teacher's role includes introducing the text, prompting during reading, reinforcing strategies and skills, and focusing and extending discussion.

In today's world of full-day kindergarten, there is more space in the curriculum for a balance of whole-class, small-group, and individual instruction, along with higher expectations for literacy development before first grade. However, the research on guided reading in kindergarten is sparse, and the practice varies. Some districts begin small-group reading instruction early in the school year, while others wait until midyear, allowing time for students to build foundational skills and teachers to build classroom routines. In many cases, it is left to the teacher's professional judgment to determine each student's readiness for small-group reading instruction, and in some districts guided reading still remains outside the structures of kindergarten. There is no single right answer for every student, every teacher, and every classroom. What we teachers do know, however, is that we don't need to wait until students have mastered concepts of print and letter-sound relations before putting a book in their hands. We know that the sooner students are provided with appropriate materials and teaching, the more likely they are to make gains in reading (NICHD, 2000).

When we work with small groups, we are better able to identify students' strengths and needs and to provide "just-in-time" teaching to meet those needs. Some groups of students will be ready to decode words on their own; others will just be figuring out where to begin reading on the page. By the end of the year, if not the beginning, many kindergartners will be reading books with a story line, two or more characters, and several lines of print on the page. We are doing our students a disservice if we fail to provide opportunities for all of them to grow as readers. Small-group reading instruction, or guided reading, is one tool for providing those opportunities—as long as we accept that guided reading may not look the quite same for emergent readers as it does for any other stage of literacy development.

> Guided reading with needs-based groups is only one type of grouping structure. Students also need opportunities to participate in interest-based, self-selected, and random groupings.

The last decade has provided extensive research to support guided reading, which has been identified as one of the most important best practices in contemporary reading instruction (Fawson & Reutzel, 2000) and has been shown to be an appropriate research-based strategy for students working on developing literacy skills (Iaquinta, 2006). Individual elements of guided reading are also well supported in current research: providing scaffolded reading practice (Fountas & Pinnell, 1996) for small, needs-based, flexible groups (Tyner, 2004), using carefully selected texts at appropriate levels of difficulty (Allington, 2009). Guided reading practices as part of a balanced literacy program conform to the recommendations suggested in position statements by IRA and the NAEYC (1998).

Organization and Management: What Are the Other Kids Doing?

Let's face it: It's unrealistic to expect to have a small-group reading program up and running at full speed in the first few weeks of school in *any* grade, much less kindergarten. We can't start working with small groups until the rest of the students are working productively and independently. So instead of feeling guilty about it, we should focus on taking as much time as is needed to establish the routines for students' independent learning, which will probably take at least six to eight weeks.

Any independent routine is appropriate for the rest of the class during small-group reading instruction as long as it is curriculum based and focused on student learning.

> A large collection of literacy center activities for kindergarten may be found at www.fcrr.org/Curriculum/studentCenterActivities.shtm.

Learning centers, more fully described in Chapter 4, have long been a popular structure for independent learning in kindergarten classrooms and beyond (see Figure 8.2). These might be dramatic play or exploration centers, but many teachers prefer—or are required by their districts—to occupy all students with a literacy-based activity during the literacy block. Literacy

Figure 8.2
Literacy Centers Provide Opportunities for Independent Practice
of Reading Skills and Strategies

center activities might include reading around the room, reading from leveled books in browsing boxes, building words from magnetic letters, playing matching games with words and pictures, or writing cards and letters to classmates. Because the structure of literacy centers lends itself so well to letter and word activities, we need to ensure there are also plenty of opportunities for connected reading and writing. One disadvantage of centers is that they often are labor intensive for us teachers. Any activity that takes more time for a teacher to prepare than it does for students to complete is a questionable use of time for both!

That's why more and more teachers are opting for learning *routines* rather than *activities*. What's the difference? Routines are habits of mind that are self-directed and self-monitored, as opposed to teacher-created, isolated activities. Literacy routines are usually based on reading and writing, such as independent reading, buddy reading, computer reading, or free-choice writing. The key is that literacy routines don't require regular preparation (or invention) on the part of the teacher and, most important, lend themselves to differentiated learning and self-regulation.

Whatever structure we use for independent learning, it's important to take time to model, demonstrate, and practice what we want students to ultimately do independently. Only one routine should be taught at a time, and no new experiences should be introduced until all students have mastered the previous one. Based on the model of the gradual release of responsibility developed by David Pearson and Margaret Gallagher (1983), the process begins with modeling and demonstrating the desired behaviors. Anchor charts serve as reminders of what those behaviors look and sound like (see Figure 8.3). Students then practice the behaviors, starting with brief, timed periods (even just one minute at first), and gradually increasing their stamina to the 15–20 minutes needed for a small-group reading session. Gail Boushey and Joan Moser (2006) call this process "building muscle memory" (p. 37).

Fifteen minutes—or more—of uninterrupted, self-monitored reading in kindergarten? It may sound like the impossible dream, but it is absolutely possible and is happening in kindergarten classrooms everywhere. Also, there is no point in starting any kind of small-group instruction until students are used to this independence.

It may take a couple of months to get everyone reading independently for 15 minutes, but once that routine is established, we teachers have 15 minutes of freedom to use for assessment, instruction, or intervention. Not to mention the fact that when we don't have to plan activities to keep the rest of the class occupied during guided reading, we can dedicate our limited planning time to what really matters—teaching.

Once we know that the other students in their class can function productively and independently for 15 minutes, we can start to work with one guided reading group, usually the most advanced one. (In primary grades, I suggest starting with the neediest group, but in kindergarten I usually start with the group that is most ready for reading.) Fifteen minutes seems to be optimal for small-group time, and you can even set a timer to remind yourself to keep the lesson short and focused. As the year goes on and students build stamina for independent activity, we can add another group but only after taking an activity break between groups. (And I emphasize the word *activity*. If students have been doing sedentary work for 15 minutes or more, it's time to play a game, sing a song, or simply "shake our sillies out" before returning to independent work.)

I usually find that, in balancing my literacy block with a read-aloud and shared reading, as well as writing workshop, I have time to work with two small groups a day. In some schools, reading specialists are helping teachers "push in" to take additional reading groups. In my own district, several professionals in the building often get together to work with groups. However, not every kindergarten teacher has outside support for small-group instruction. The reality is that we teachers are not going to be able to see every group every day. We will ensure, however, that every child experiences a rich program of read-alouds, shared reading, writing, and other literacy experiences every day.

In my home district, several professionals in a school often work together during small-group reading time, with the students working with each teacher over the course of the week. Each group has a different instructional focus, based on the needs of their group:

- Classroom teacher: Guided reading
- Learning support teacher: Interactive writing
- Teacher-librarian: Small-group interactive read-aloud
- Speech-language pathologist: Oral-language activities or phonemic awareness
- Paraprofessionals: Word games or scripted activities

The instructional team meets once a week to analyze and restructure groupings or to plan appropriate instruction to meet each group's needs.

Figure 8.3
Anchor Chart of Desired Behaviors

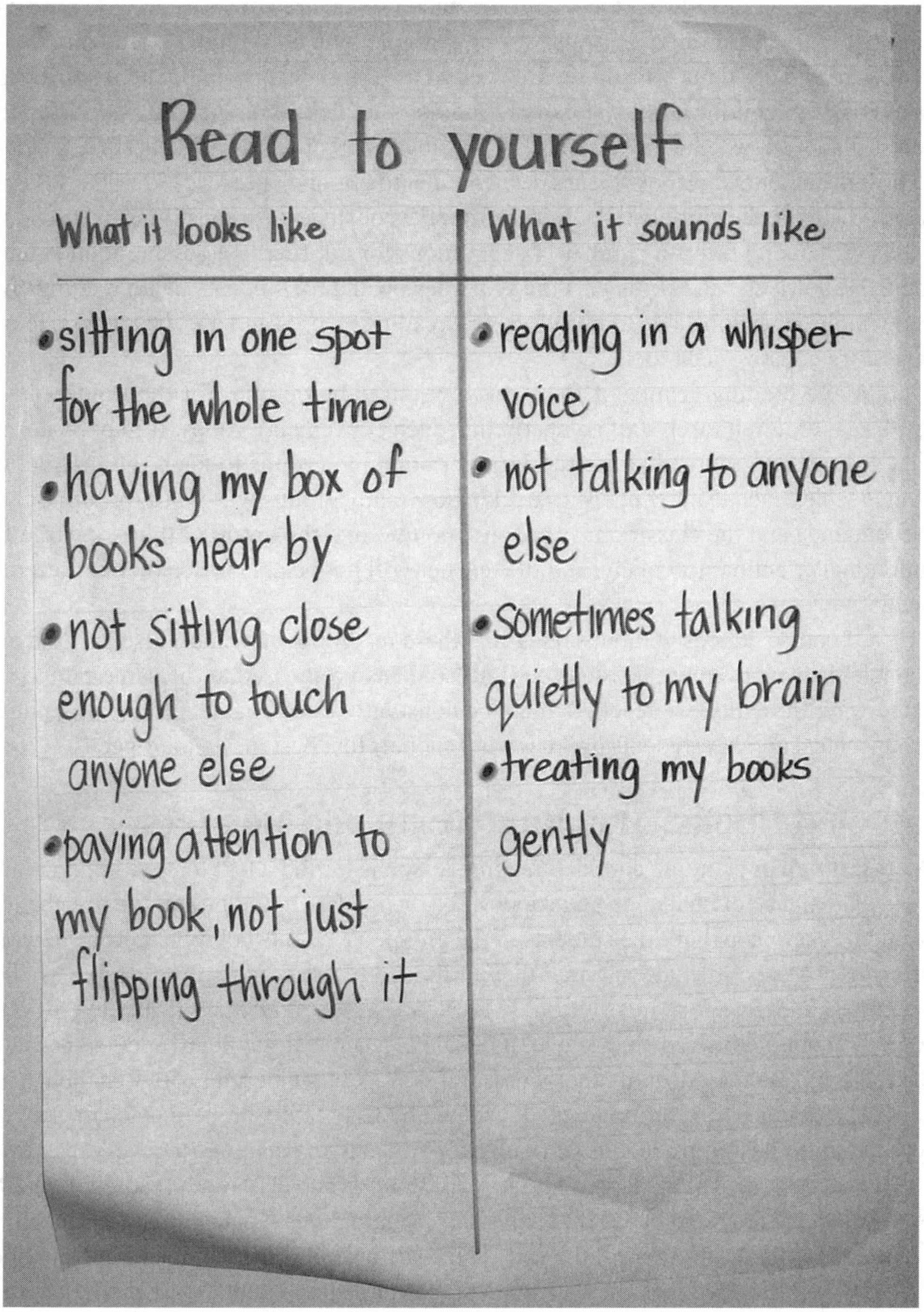

Read to yourself

What it looks like	What it sounds like
• sitting in one spot for the whole time	• reading in a whisper voice
• having my box of books near by	• not talking to anyone else
• not sitting close enough to touch anyone else	• sometimes talking quietly to my brain
• paying attention to my book, not just flipping through it	• treating my books gently

Assessment and Grouping

As students are building stamina as independent learners, we as their teachers can begin to assess knowledge of the alphabet, phonological awareness, and basic concepts of print. A running record isn't too useful for students who are not yet reading, but we can conduct many informal assessments. For example, you could hand a student a book backward and upside-down and see if the child turns it right-side up before reading. You could ask the child if he or she can distinguish the picture on a given page from the words and, if so, whether he or she can name any letters or words. Having students identify alphabet letters, write their names, and identify sounds in words are other assessments that will help establish the initial groupings of students with similar instructional needs. (Chapter 3 offers a number of suggestions for informally assessing foundational literacy knowledge and skills.) As the year goes on and the students begin reading conventionally, we will be able to introduce oral reading records and miscue analysis to our repertoire of assessment tools.

While reading groups of four or five seem to be optimal for the kindergarten level, real children rarely fall so neatly into such convenient groups. It may be necessary to split up groups that are too large or combine groups to keep the instruction manageable. Each teacher needs to decide how many groups will work for him or her, the students, and the classroom situation: Too few, and the group will be too large for individual attention; too many, and the teacher will not be able to see them as often as needed.

Of course, it goes without saying that these reading groups must also be fluid and flexible. How convenient it would be if all students progressed at the same rate in the same way! In reality, we teachers must be constantly assessing and adjusting reading groups to ensure that students are receiving support that best meets their needs.

Leveled Books: Matching Texts and Readers

A critical step in planning a guided reading lesson is to find a text that will provide just the right balance of challenge and support for the readers in the group. Ideally, the text would be easy enough for the students in the group to read most of it on their own, while offering just enough challenge that they will need to draw on reading strategies. The accepted guideline for "instructional" level is that the students will be able to read roughly 9 out of 10 words in the text and have a general, if not deep, understanding of the material (Betts, 1946). In other words, think of 90% support and 10% challenge.

The practice of leveling texts, developed by Clay (1991) to help teachers provide reading materials of graduated difficulty for students in Reading Recovery, has been adopted and adapted for use with small-group classroom reading. Leveling systems are based on analysis of print features, vocabulary, predictability, and illustrations in the text. The chart in Table 8.1 describes some qualities of leveled texts at four main stages of development. Most kindergartners will be emergent or early readers.

Guided reading has readers standing on their tiptoes, with the teacher there to balance or catch them as needed.

Table 8.1
What Leveled Texts Look Like

	For Emergent Readers	For Early Readers	For Developing Readers
What does the page look like?	• Limited amount of print on the page • Enlarged text and spaces between words • Print that is in the same place on every page • Illustrations that are heavily supportive of text	• May be two or more lines of print on the page, often enlarged and always separated from the illustrations • Illustrations that help tell the story • Lines break at meaningful chunks	• May be paragraphs of print on the page • Print sometimes found in different places on different pages and integrated with illustrations • Illustrations that enhance the story or information but text that usually stands alone
What does the language look like?	• Highly predictable and patterned language—from single words to one or two sentences	• Short sentences, mostly high-frequency and decodable words • Key vocabulary that is likely to be repeated	• More natural language, but it may be choppy due to short sentences • Less control on vocabulary, few repeated words
What is the content like?	• Realistic events and concepts to which children can relate • Text is generally labeling of pictures	• Basic story lines, often with characters and dialogue • Situations that are usually realistic • Informational text on familiar topics	• Story lines that may have a twist or unusual features • Beginnings of imaginative text or folklore, beyond the experiences of the readers

Let's remember that leveling only tells us what the text brings to the reading experience. The other factor in the equation is the reader. Does he or she have adequate background knowledge to understand the concepts in the text? Are most of the words in his or her speaking vocabulary? Will the length of the text be a motivator or a deterrent for this reader? No publisher can tell teachers that. Only through assessments and professional knowledge can we make that important match between the reader and the "just-right" text. We've all had the experience of students reading one leveled text with ease, then struggling with another text at the same level. That's why it's important for us teachers to understand the leveling criteria. It's also important to remember that "instructional level" is for instruction. We never want to limit students to reading only books at their level. Chapter 9 discusses the importance of supporting students in making choices of what they *can* and *want* to read for independent reading.

The Guided Reading Lesson: The Nuts and Bolts

The guided reading lesson is a fine balance between careful planning and seizing the teachable moment. Good teaching should always begin with the end in mind: What do I want my students to take from this lesson? A lesson may focus on one or more specific comprehension or word-solving behaviors, or on using a repertoire of comprehension and word-solving strategies to access a text. This is not a time for the introduction of new strategies or lots of teacher talk. This brief period should be focused on student reading and talking about their reading. In planning an integrated guided reading lesson, I suggest trying to address one comprehension (text-level) strategy and one word-level strategy. (Sample lessons for emergent and early readers are found later in this chapter.)

Once you've determined the lesson focus, choose a text that will be at an appropriate level of difficulty for the group and lends itself to the learning goal. (This is not as difficult as it may seem: Almost any book can be used for letter identification or long vowel sounds.)

Before Reading

The book introduction may very well be the teacher's most important task in the guided reading cycle. A strong book introduction is intended to provide just enough support to prime the pump, enabling students to tackle the text and apply their strategies with a degree of independence. As with a read-aloud lesson (described in Chapter 6), you can use the 3 Ps: (1) preview, (2) prior knowledge, and (3) purpose for reading.

> The book introduction is the bridge between the reader and the text. When planning a book introduction, consider the 3 Ps:
> 1. Preview
> 2. Prior knowledge
> 3. Purpose

For the preview, introduce the title and author, provide a one-sentence overview of what the book is about, and picture walk some or all of the pages in the book. When we activate students' prior knowledge, we want students to think about what they already know about the topic or story so they can anticipate what the story will be about and make connections as they read. Sometimes, you may find it necessary to do some preteaching (another P) of vocabulary and concepts. Finally, articulate the purpose for the reading: What do we hope to learn or find out, what strategies are we going to use, and what should we look for in the text?

> A picture walk, or "pic flic," is a page-by-page preview of the illustrations in the book, intended to give students an overview of what the book is about.

During Reading

During the guided reading lesson, students are usually reading on their own, not in unison or taking turns, round-robin style. That's why it's important that every student has his or her own copy of the text. This process is made more challenging by the fact that kindergartners can't read silently! Some teachers provide "reading phones" made of PVC pipe (see Figure 8.4) to help keep students' voices down. Another idea is to stagger start the reading so the students aren't all reading the same page at the same time. Remind them that when they come to the end of the book, they should flip right back to the front and read it again. In fact, encourage them to see how many times they can read the book before you tell them to stop. While students are reading, listen to each student for a brief few moments and provide support as needed.

After Reading

After reading, extend students' strategies and experience with the text by talking about what they read; retelling the story; and revisiting the text to focus on individual words, letters, and sounds. In this way, we begin with the whole text before isolating language

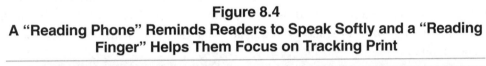

Figure 8.4
A "Reading Phone" Reminds Readers to Speak Softly and a "Reading Finger" Helps Them Focus on Tracking Print

elements, applying the whole-part-whole principle considered to be a best practice in literacy instruction (Morrow & Asbury, 2003). Beginning level texts usually don't have much metacognitive meat to chew on, but we can reflect on the various word-solving actions students might have used to access an unfamiliar word. If the text lends itself to extended or inferential thinking, prompt students to explain their ideas or refer to the text to support their thinking. I suggest you conclude the reading with a shared or interactive writing lesson in an effort to make that all-important reading–writing connection.

Needless to say, the 15-minute time frame is usually over before we teachers will have completed this lesson sequence, and we will need to continue working with the same text during the next session. Ideally, we will always spend at least two days with any one book, and sometimes more, depending on the richness of the text.

The Must-Do

After completing a lesson sequence, the students add the book to their individual book boxes and complete a "must-do"—an assigned task that extends the students' experiences with the text or provides independent practice on a skill or strategy on which the lesson focused. The "must-do" might involve word hunts, games, word sorts, picture-writing tasks (Figure 8.5), or reading with a buddy. After all, the whole point of the guided reading lesson is for students to transfer what they have learned to their own independent reading.

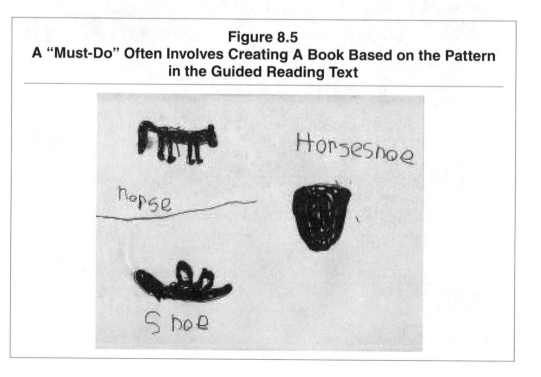

Figure 8.5
A "Must-Do" Often Involves Creating A Book Based on the Pattern in the Guided Reading Text

Guided Reading for Emergent Readers

Many, if not most, kindergartners will be considered emergent readers, at least at the beginning of the school year. They may know a lot of things about books and stories and may even role-play reading, but they are not yet negotiating print. Some teachers believe that students at this stage are not ready for guided reading; however, I believe that we teachers can accelerate concepts of print, letters, and sounds by providing appropriate books and support to students even before conventional reading begins.

At this emergent stage, the guided reading lesson is something like a modified shared reading lesson, using little books rather than Big Books or other enlarged print (see sample lesson in Figure 8.6). These learners read from pictures and memory. That's why texts at this stage must be highly predictable and patterned, with strong picture support. At the lowest levels, there is only one word on each page, usually labeling the illustration. As the texts increase in difficulty, there may be phrases or even entire sentences on each page, and the predictable pattern may change on the last page of the book. Eventually readers will be expected to sweep their eyes from the end of one line to the beginning of the next as two lines begin to appear on the page, though these lines are still heavily patterned.

Tools for guided reading at this stage include
- Books
- "Reading fingers"
- Trackers and framers
- Sets of alphabet letters
- Name bags
- Alphabet chart or place mat

At higher levels, we teachers don't read aloud the whole text for the students because they are expected to access the print on their own. For emergent readers, however, it's the only way to make that initial acquaintance with what the text says. Start by presenting the 3 Ps book introduction and a picture walk through the entire book. In this way, you can make sure that there are no unfamiliar words in the text. Then, holding the book up for the students to see and tracking each word with a finger, read each page expressively and fluently (something of a challenge when there are only one or two words on the page).

After the book introduction, the books are distributed so each student has his or her own copy from which to read. Ensuring that each child has a book in his or her hands is an important part of guided reading. I often provide the students with "reading fingers." ("Witch fingers" such as the ones in Figure 8.4, are available from any dollar store at Halloween.) The students can read the text chorally with you, tracking each word and turning the pages together. After the text has been read several times (and the students have essentially memorized the words), they can go back and "read" it themselves—over and over and over again. Together with you, they can finally revisit this memorized text to match words, isolate letters, look for patterns, and reinforce voice-print matching. That's where the reading manipulatives come in. Giving students trackers (anything with a point, such as chopsticks or stir sticks) and framers (anything with a hole, such as a magnifying glass or a ring) turns the word work into play (see Figure 8.7).

In addition to negotiating connected text, we should work with students on sounds, letters, and words at the emergent level (see Figure 8.8 for activity suggestions). As much

---

Figure 8.6
Sample Guided Reading Sequence for Emergent Readers

GROUP: Emergent **DATE:**   **TEXT:** A Sun, a Flower **LEVEL:** 2

Text-Level Focus	*Word-Level Focus*
• Using pictures and letters to read	• Identifying letters of the alphabet
• Tracking words and understanding directionality	• Recognizing beginning and ending sounds
• Understanding compound words	• Isolating and matching words

BOOK INTRO *Preview* *Prior Knowledge* *Purpose*	*This is a book about special kinds of words—compound words.* *What do you get when you put sun and flower together?* *What other words can you put together?* *Let's read to see what other words the author put together.* *I think you will be able to read this whole book by yourself.* *See how many times you can read this book before I tell you to stop.* *When I tap your book, please read more loudly for me to listen.*

DAY 1	**Must-Do**
• Provide book introduction and preview. • Do page-by-page picture walk ("pic flic"). • Read aloud the text to the students, modeling and tracking. • Distribute copies of the book and read in unison. • Have students read independently, using tracking. • Talk about what they read • Sound—picture match: Put your finger on a word that starts with k. Put your finger on a word that ends with p. • Print-matching detectives: "This word says basketball. Be a word detective and find the word basketball in your book with your magnifying glass. How do you know it says basketball? I'm going to show you a word card, but I'm not going to tell you what this word says. See if you can be a word detective and find it in your book and tell me what the word is.	• Buddy read the entire book, taking turns reading page by page. • Provide a set of phrases from the text on word cards, and have students match the word cards to the words in the book.
DAY 2	**Must-Do**
• Have students reread text independently as teacher listens. • Review the word-matching must-do activity. • Play letter hunt: Be a word detective and find a letter T,, for example. • Do shared/interactive writing: Brainstorm compound words.	• Make your own compound word book.

Figure 8.7
Simon Points Out "Star Words" With a Star-Shaped Swizzle Stick

Figure 8.8
Possible Activities for Emergent Readers in Guided Reading Groups

Phonemic Awareness Activities:	Letter Identification Activities:	Name Activities:
• Clap the syllables in words from the text.	• Be detectives and hunt for specific letters in the text.	• Provide each student with a bag containing the letters in his or her own name to sort or compare.
• Generate rhymes for words from the text.	• Provide each student with an alphabet placemat. Have students track and read the letters in different ways: taking turns, making funny voices, tracking just the red letters or the blue letters, and so on.	• Have students "mix and fix" their own name.
• Think of words that begin or end with the same sound as key words from the text.		• Name or draw a letter, and have students indicate whether or not it's in their name.
• Blend and segment words from the text	• Play games like drawing plastic letters out of a bag and naming them. Play "hot potato letters" by naming the letter as quickly as possible and dropping it back in the bag or on the table.	• Choose a word from the text. Ask students to compare it with the letters in their own name.
• Manipulate words by changing beginning, ending, or medial sounds (sat to cat or sack or sit).		
• Use Elkonin boxes or train cars to represent beginning, middle, and ending sounds in words.	• Say a letter and have students point to it or find it in a letter pile	

97

NOTES

as possible, use the letters and words in the book as the context for phonemic awareness and phonics practice. This is where the areas of skill focus are differentiated.

Must-do activities for emergent readers are always connected to the lesson focus and might include the following:

- Make your own book using the pattern from the text.

- Read the book with a buddy, taking turns reading each page.

- Sort pictures for the letter or sound focus of the lesson.

- Work with a partner to sort alphabet letters by letters in each name, letters in both names, or letters in neither name.

- Go "fishing" for magnetic letters, and name the letters you catch.

Guided Reading for Early Readers

Once students can write their own names, have a pretty solid mastery of concepts of print and sounds in words, and know the letter names and sounds, they are considered *early* readers. Figure 8.9 provides a sample guided reading lesson for early readers.

Because these readers are making letter-sound connections, they are starting to be able to negotiate print on their own. This is why early level texts no longer need to be heavily patterned. These texts tend to have more natural language and illustrations that support the ideas more than the vocabulary. There is often dialogue between two characters. New vocabulary is usually reinforced several times in the text. Because we as teachers want to encourage readers at this stage to read in phrases, rather than word by word, line breaks in the text occur at meaningful phrases, rather than at the end of the space. Here's the opportunity to put away the "reading fingers" and replace them with "sliders" (such as short rulers) to slide under each line (see Figure 8.10).

At this point, students should negotiate the text themselves in guided reading groups. We shouldn't read aloud the text to them or invite them to read in chorus. However, we should still present the 3 Ps book introduction. Take the students on a picture walk of some or all of the illustrations or invite them to do their own picture walk and "talk to your brain about what you see in the pictures." If some of the vocabulary presents a challenge, you could preteach critical words by "building" them with magnetic letters or making connections to known words.

After the 3 Ps book introduction, give the books to the students for them to read independently. As the students read, listen to each one for a few moments and provide scaffolding and support for miscues. The challenge is allowing students time for self-corrections. All too often, we teachers intervene before students even spit the whole words out of their mouths. Instead, count for at least three seconds—or until the reader gets to the end of the page—to give the child time to realize a word was incorrect. If the student doesn't self-correct, then guide him or her by asking questions like these:

Vocabulary: To Preteach or Not to Preteach?

- Is the word critical to understanding a key point in the text? We don't want to take a chance on students missing the word.

- Should the students be able to word solve the word on their own? If it's not decodable or otherwise easy to figure out, we'd better preteach it.

- Is the word interesting but not essential to the reading? Give the students a chance to solve it on their own and revisit it after reading to talk about strategies a reader might use.

Figure 8.9
Sample Guided Reading Sequence for Early Readers

GROUP: Early   **DATE:**   **TEXT:** *All Clean*   **LEVEL:** *8*

Text-Level Focus	*Word-Level Focus*
• Self-monitoring: using meaning, sound, and visual cues • Understanding unique text structure: speech bubble • Reading in phrases: fluency • Retelling: story structure	• Using chunks to help decode • Reviewing high-frequency word review for automaticity • Identifying word endings

BOOK INTRO *Preview Prior Knowledge Purpose*	*This is a book about a lady named Marion who loves to clean her house. How will you notice the name Marion? What do you notice on the cover? The bird is called a parrot. How will you know if you see the word parrot in the book?* *Tell your partner about a time you helped clean up.* *As I reveal this word, one letter at a time, try to guess what it is.* *Here is a word you'll see in the book we're about to read: clean. Let's use these magnetic letters to build other words that end with –ean.* *This circle is called a speech bubble. How do you think the parrot would sound? We've been talking about asking yourself three questions when you read: Does this make sense? Does it sound right? Does it look right? As you read today, I want you to talk to your brain about these three questions to make sure you read the words that are on the page.* *See how many times you can read this book before I tell you to stop.* *When I tap your book, please read more loudly for me to listen.*

DAY 1	**Must-Do**
• Provide book introduction and vocabulary preview. • Model reading with sliders, instead of tracking. • Have students read independently, self-monitoring and phrasing. • Ask after reading, *What do you think?* • Ask a "big idea" question: *Could this really happen?* • Revisit speech bubbles: *What do you think the parrot is saying? What do you think Marion would say?*	• Have students do buddy reading, and after each person takes a turn reading a page, the listener must retell what was read on that page, as a comprehension check. • Have students generate and illustrate –ean words and then write a silly rhyme using at least two of the words (e.g., "My friend Dean ate a bean.").
DAY 2	**Must-Do**
• Reread text independently. • Review must-do activity. • Play a retelling game or create a retelling map (see Chapter 6). • Model self-monitoring by reading sentences with an obvious error, such as "Marion cleaned the vacuum's feathers." Ask students to explain what's wrong, how they know it's wrong, and how they would fix it.	• Draw and label: What happened at the beginning, in the middle, at the end?
DAY 3	**Must-Do**
• Have students read the text independently. • Review must-do (share). • Have students be word detectives to find endings: -ing, -ed, -s, -er. • Identify c-blend words	• Write around the room: Hunt for -ed, -ing, and -s words. Read the words to a partner.

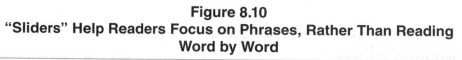

Figure 8.10
"Sliders" Help Readers Focus on Phrases, Rather Than Reading
Word by Word

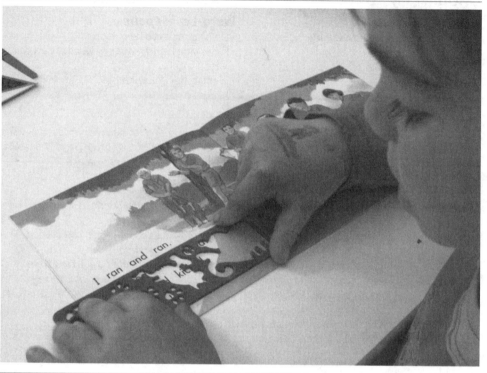

- *Does that word make sense?* If not, invite students to use their other cueing systems to help them read a word that makes sense. Remind students that making sense is the most important part of reading.

- *Does that word sound right?* If the word doesn't sound right in oral language, that's a sign that it's not the right word.

  - *Does that word look right?* The final cue is to look at whether the word matches the print. Is that the right beginning or ending sound?

After the reading, it's important to reinforce word-solving strategies that the students used during reading. For example, invite students to retell the story or information. (A range of retelling activities may be found in Chapter 6.) Asking "What do you think about the book?" or prompting students with a "big idea" question is a simple way to get their responses.

The second day with the text should always begin with an independent rereading. Sometimes we might take a quick running record or simply listen to each student read and offer support as needed. Playing a brief game to

Teaching children to self-monitor their reading is important at this stage since they sometimes breeze through miscues without correcting them.
Remind children that every word they read must do the following:

- Make sense
- Sound right
- Match the print

reinforce high-frequency words or key vocabulary from the text is another option for day two. As with emergent readers, early readers should revisit the text to focus on letters, words, and patterns as needed. Other recommended activities are highlighting high-frequency words, looking at word families, and building words. Spend the last five minutes of the lesson on a guided writing task such as a dictated or open-ended sentence. Some small-group activities for early readers may be found in Figure 8.11.

After the lesson, some must-do activities might include the following:

- Write around the room: Students tour the room with a clipboard, writing any words they find that meet specific criteria related to the word work from the story, such as words ending in *s* or words with double letters.

- Reinforce high-frequency words: Provide letter stamps or magnetic letters for the students to read each word chosen from the story, build it, and then write it on paper or a magnetic whiteboard (see page 154).

- Copycat stories: Have students write their own stories based on the story they read in the group.

- Read some more: Provide a book on a similar topic or by the same author as the story read in the group but at a slightly easier reading level.

Figure 8.11
Possible Activities for Early Readers in Guided Reading Groups

Comprehension Activities:	Fluency Activities:	Word-Solving Activities:
• Play retelling games (see Chapter 6).	• Move a slider under each line of text to read in phrases.	• Mix and fix with magnetic letters or letter tiles.
• "Talk to your brain" (self-talk during reading).	• Talk like the talker (expression in dialogue).	• Perform word and letter hunts in the text.
• Ask three questions (self-monitoring).	• Pause at the period.	• Build "ladders" of rhyming words.
• Use comprehension gestures (see Chapter 6).		• Karate-chop the word into parts.
		• Play Read My Mind (students guess a hidden word as one letter is revealed at a time).
		• Play Vowel Sound Bingo.
		• Read around the word (context clues).
		• Look for parts you know.

Never before has differentiating reading instruction been more critical. We teachers are dealing with increasing ranges of student skill and ability, varying amounts of oral-language development, and huge differences in the amount of literacy experiences kindergartners bring to school with them. Some children arrive at the classroom door already knowing how to negotiate print and make meaning from books. Others may, in spite of innate intelligence, have simply had limited opportunities to interact with books or even build oral-language skills. We as educators have always known that one size doesn't fit all in reading instruction. Guided reading, as one part of a balanced literacy program, helps us fit every student.

CHAPTER 9

"We Can Read!": The Power of Independent Reading

Emily and Danika sit on the floor with their heads bent over a simple alphabet picture book. They take turns naming the picture on each page: *apple, butterfly, crayon, dragon.* As they reach the final picture—*zipper*—Danika exclaims, "We can read!" When children see themselves as readers and writers, it is a foundational step in their journey to literacy.

It's never too early to begin to foster recreational reading habits. Research shows that the amount of leisure time spent reading is an excellent predictor of and, in fact, a causal factor in children's growth in reading and vocabulary (Fielding, Wilson, & Anderson, 1986). Starting from kindergarten, children who read more perform better on literacy assessments and measures of general knowledge (Lapp, Flood, & Roser, 2000). Allington (2009) cites extensive research to support the importance of "reading volume"; in other words, the more you read, the better you get at reading.

Morrow (1991) found that one of the main features in classrooms where children frequently chose to read independently was an attractive and accessible classroom library. The reading corner is the focal point of many kindergarten classrooms, often doubling as a gathering place for morning meetings, read-alouds, modeled writing, and other large-group activities. Soft cushions, private nooks and crannies, and plenty of books of all types and genres make the reading corner comfortable and accessible, a desirable spot for free-choice activity. Scour yard sales for an old upholstered chair or sofa and ask for carpet remnants at flooring stores to make the reading corner cozy. Placing the reading corner near a window will ensure there will be plenty of light. Try to find ways to create individual spaces; for example, a packing box from a new appliance makes a great book nook. A talented volunteer might be able to build a reading loft or sew beanbag chairs or oversized pillows. I've seen wonderfully inviting kindergarten reading corners containing tents, bunk beds, and even electric fireplaces. Add some literature-based dramatic play props such as puppets, costumes, and dolls, and you'll have a reading corner that the children won't be able to resist.

Classroom libraries should have these characteristics:

- Be attractive and visible, a focal point of the classroom
- Be partitioned and private to allow quiet reading space
- Contain comfortable seating, if possible, or at the very least, a carpeted area to sit on
- Contain a range of styles and genres of books and other print materials
- Have books displayed with covers facing out
- Include literature-based displays and props such as puppets or books on tape
- Have an organizational structure that children can relate to

(Fractor, Woodruff, Martinez, & Teale, 1993)

Morrow (1997) also recommends that the classroom library contain 8 to 10 books per child. Although regular visits to school and public libraries are important, research has shown that children who have access to books in the classroom read up to 50% more than students in classrooms without libraries (Bissett, 1969). Martinez and Teale (1988) found that emergent readers are more likely to choose books that are predictable and familiar to them. In fact, they reported that the books kindergartners are most likely to try to read conventionally are the Big Books that have been read and reread during shared reading. Any time you read aloud a book, place it in the reading corner for students to visit again. A rule of thumb is to change about one-third of the books each month, though special favorites may be kept on display longer, even for the entire school year.

Walk into any bookstore and you are likely to notice marketing tricks for attracting consumers to the books: an organizational structure that is easy to navigate, books organized by theme or author, special displays that are changed regularly, and featured books with covers facing out. The same rules apply to the kindergarten library. Books in the kindergarten classroom library should be stored within easy reach of students, with plenty of book covers on display (see Figure 9.1). One clever way to display books is in plastic rain gutters mounted low on the classroom walls.

The reading materials in the classroom library should represent a whole range of genres: stories, poetry, informational texts, Big Books, folk and fairy tales, and

Figure 9.1
A Classroom Library Displaying Books Within Easy Reach

class- and student-made books. Many teachers store books in baskets or tubs by topic, genre, or level and identify each group with a distinctive sticker to guide students to return the books to the correct tub. I have a special trunk for "theme books" that I've gathered from public, school, and personal libraries to support a featured topic of study.

Why not invite the students to help organize the classroom library? Teacher Katie DiCesare (2008) describes how she and her students came up with categories such as Books That Are Good for Picture Reading, Song Books, Rhyming Books, Books We Can Read Ourselves, and Books We've Read Aloud, as well as books organized by author and theme.

What Kinds of Books Do Kindergarten Children Read?

Choice is a key to engaging kindergartners in reading (Lapp et al., 2000). When students have a variety of books accessible to them, they are more likely to spend time interacting with those books. They enjoy revisiting books that have been read in the classroom. They take delight in class-made books to which they've contributed. It's very important for young children to see their lives reflected in the books they read; be sure to include a range of cultures and family structures in the collection.

Trade books (books published and sold for general use, as opposed to educational books) often have interesting story lines, beautiful illustrations, and rich language, but these books are usually too difficult for emerging readers to read independently. Leveled books, usually "little books," are designed specifically to support growing readers at various stages of development, but they do little to enrich a child's imagination or background knowledge. There is room in the kindergarten library for both types of books.

Have We Teachers Gone Loony Over Leveling?

The practice of leveling texts was originally developed by Clay (1991) to provide reading materials of graduated difficulty for Reading Recovery. Today, these little books are ubiquitous in primary classrooms as tools for guided reading instruction and independent reading practice. They are often organized by level in tubs or browsing boxes for student selection. In some classrooms, students are restricted to reading only books at their level, and some librarians are required to order only books that have been leveled according to one formula or another. (See Chapter 8 for more information on leveling books for guided reading instruction.) Before we teachers get too loony over leveling, we need to remember that any leveling system can only tell us what the book brings to the reading equation; it cannot predict the interests, background experience, and motivation of the reader. Books are leveled, not children! We need to ensure that students have a range of types and levels of books at their disposal to help them develop the very important life skill of choosing books they *can* and *want to* read.

I'm not suggesting that we prevent students from reading just-right books, but maybe it's time to expand the definition of just-right books for

> "I worry that if our kids are limited to just-right books 100 percent of the time in our classrooms, they may not learn the possibilities and promise of reading, nor will they easily develop their own goals and plans as readers that are more personal than moving to the next reading level."
>
> *(Collins, 2008, p. 72)*

independent reading to include more challenging books that capture a student's interest and engagement. By the same token, banning leveled little books from the school library pretty much ensures that there will be no books for emergent and early readers to read conventionally. For many children, it's incredibly empowering to be able to select books in which they can actually negotiate the print. Why not make leveled books *available* to students for self-selected reading but not *limit* students to reading books at their independent or instructional reading level? These books do not have to be numbered or otherwise identified by level; however, a range of little books could be integrated into a theme trunk or the general classroom collection.

In some classrooms where "read to yourself" is an independent learning option during the reading block, teachers may feel compelled (or mandated) to limit student reading to books that support students' abilities to build decoding skills. In this case, it would be useful to schedule another part of the day for self-selected reading. Perhaps it's possible to squeeze in some "library" periods each week. Some teachers use morning arrival time for free-choice reading; others find free-choice reading an effective quiet transition after outdoor play. One advantage to scheduling independent reading times that are separate from the literacy instruction block is that the teacher is not occupied with small-group teaching and can circulate freely among the students to make observations and assessments and take a few minutes to confer with students about what they are reading.

Book Boxes

Individual book boxes are one way to ensure that every student has a range of reading materials at his or her fingertips at all times. Cardboard or plastic magazine storage boxes work well for individual book boxes because they hold a range of book sizes and store neatly on a shelf. In each student's book box should be a collection of texts that include the last four or five guided reading texts, a sampling of little books chosen to be at the student's independent reading level, and two or three picture books that he or she has chosen based on interest, rather than degree of difficulty. A student's book box may also contain a folder of class poems that have been read together during shared reading and some little books that he or she has created in response to reading.

> Independent-level text is considered to be at the level a child needs for reading practice on his or her own. The reader should be able to read virtually 100% of the words and comprehend the text thoroughly.

At the beginning of the year, we teachers provide strong support and may even choose the books for the students' book boxes, but over the course of the year, we want to gradually release responsibility to the students to select their own books. The materials in these book boxes may be changed once a week or more frequently, depending on the students and the class situation.

Finding Books That Are Accessible to Emergent Readers

Although most trade books were not written to be read independently by five-year-olds, there are many types of books that do support these young readers. Strong illustrations, familiar topics, or recurring characters or themes are features that make books accessible. In the classroom library or school library, we teachers can support by creating displays of favorite authors, themes, or genres (e.g., fairy tales, alphabet books, wordless picture books, information books, and how-to books). Introduce students to books with familiar characters and plot structures, such as Charlie and Lola (Lauren Child), Scaredy Squirrel (Mélanie Watt), Llama Llama (Anna Dewdney), Olivia (Ian Falconer), Fancy Nancy (Jane O'Connor), Franklin the Turtle (Paulette Bourgeois), and, of course, the irrepressible David (David Shannon). Other supports include predictable or patterned text, which is often accompanied by rhythm and rhyme, such as *Brown Bear, Brown Bear, What Do You See?* (Bill Martin Jr), *If You Give a Mouse a Cookie* (Laura Numeroff), *Mortimer* (Robert Munsch), *The Jacket I Wear in the Snow* (Shirley Neitzel), or *Are You My Mother?* (P. D. Eastman).

How Kindergartners Read: A Reality Check

It is too much to expect most kindergartners to focus on one book for an extended period of time. Janet Hickman (1981) found that the most common activities among kindergarten and first-grade students during independent reading time were browsing and flipping through books. Let's face it: It is also unrealistic to expect silence during independent reading time in kindergarten. Most students prefer to connect with others as they interact

with books, and even those who read alone are likely to verbalize aloud as they read. In fact, Ann Forester and Margaret Reinhard (1989) admit that "once it was acknowledged that Uninterrupted Sustained Silent Reading was neither silent nor uninterrupted, and consisted of little actual reading, we simply called it book time" (p. 56).

Kindergartners do engage with books in a variety of ways, however. In Elizabeth Sulzby's (1985) classic study, she noted that children go through a set of predictable stages in their ability to acquire meaning from books. Long before they can actually decode the words, children who have a rich literacy background are able to "pretend read," turning pages of a book and telling the story using the words and expressions of "book language." Sulzby identifies the following stages in storybook retelling:

• At the least sophisticated level, the child simply labels or responds to the pictures on each page, with no evidence of understanding that the pictures connect to a story.

• At the next level, the child actually creates his or her own story, using the pictures in the book and his or her own background experience.

• Eventually, a transition is made between oral and written language, and the child creates a story that is influenced by the text in the book. It may include patterns or even phrases from the actual text.

- By this time, the child may refuse to try to read at all, because he or she has begun to understand enough about the reading process to know that he or she is not able to read all of the words conventionally.

- Finally, the child begins to make sense of the print, using a variety of strategies to decode words and comprehend text.

Knowledge of the ways young children interact with text and the developmental progression from browsing to accessing print can help teachers nurture emerging readers and support student engagement at all stages of development.

Getting Started With Independent Reading

As with all classroom activities, it is necessary to establish routines and clarify expectations for students during independent reading time. We teachers can model the appropriate behaviors and create an anchor chart that describes what independent reading looks and sounds like. The first procedural lesson I teach is "How to Read in Kindergarten." Based on Sulzby's research, I tell my students that there are three different ways that we read in kindergarten: (1) Sometimes we just look at the pictures and "talk to our brains" about what we see in the pictures, (2) sometimes we make up our own story to go along with the pictures, and (3) sometimes we read the words. It all depends on the book because different books require different ways to read. I think aloud as I model the three different ways to read (see Figure 9.2). Then I invite the students to try each of the techniques. While the students are gathered together, I provide each student with his or her own book, and they practice talking to their brains about what they see in the pictures. When I'm confident that they can all do this step, I invite them to make up a story to go along with the pictures in the book. I tell them they might start with "Once there was a..." and tell themselves a story to go along with the illustrations. (This is more challenging for students who have not had a rich storytelling background at home.) At this point, most kindergartners do not have a repertoire of books that they can read conventionally, but I tell them that soon they will have lots of books in which they can read the words.

At this point, it's time to practice building students' reading stamina. I provide each student with two or three little books and place the students around the room in individual reading spots. (Later, I will teach them about finding their own reading spot, but for now, I want them strategically placed where they will not be able to interfere with others.) As Boushey and Moser (2006) suggest, we start with a two-minute timeframe. I set the timer, and at the end of the two minutes, we all return to the carpet to self-evaluate the "read to yourself" time. However, if any student behaves inappropriately during the timeframe, we stop the reading and everyone returns to the meeting place to self-evaluate and revisit the anchor chart of appropriate behaviors. The next day, we will try again for two minutes and again and again until *everyone* can meet the desired objective. Only then will we move on to three minutes and four and beyond.

Figure 9.2
A Vignette: "How We Read in Kindergarten"

Sixteen kindergartners gather on the carpet around me. Using *Somebody and the Three Blairs*, by Marilyn Tolhurst, a favorite read-aloud, I demonstrate the "three ways to read in kindergarten." "Sometimes when we read, we read the pictures," I tell the students. Then I think aloud about the illustrations in the book. "Here's a family in their kitchen. I see a mom, a dad, and a little kid. Oh, look. In this picture it looks like a big teddy bear is opening the door." Together, we talk about the things we see in the illustrations before we move on.

"Sometimes, we make up our own story to go with the pictures: 'Once upon a time, there was a mom, a dad, and a little kid who went for a walk. Suddenly, a big teddy bear opened their door and came right into their house.'" I create a simple story line based on the illustrations.

"And sometimes, we can read the words: 'Baby Blair's chair was just right.'"

"That's how we read in kindergarten: Sometimes we read the pictures, sometimes we read the words, and sometimes we make up our own story."

I give each student a book, and we all practice "talking to our brains" about the pictures in our books. Then we all practice making up a story about the pictures. Finally, I ask the students if there are any words they can read in their books. Obviously, at the beginning of the year, their "reading" will be heavily weighted toward illustrations, but as the students build a repertoire of letters, sounds, and high-frequency words, as well as a collection of leveled books, the balance will increasingly tip toward reading the words and pictures.

Some teachers create a daily graph as a visual representation of the length of independent reading time. It may take several weeks, but using this system of clear expectations, sensitive scaffolding, and successive approximation, every kindergartner can learn to interact with books for 15 minutes. The time spent practicing is well worthwhile. Not only do students learn to engage with books for extended time periods but also the teacher is freed up to conduct small-group instruction, individual assessments, or reading conferences.

This system of modeling appropriate behavior, ensuring that all students are capable of the behavior, giving students supported opportunities to practice and master the behavior, and making students accountable for the behavior may be used for many classroom routines and procedures. Some additional lessons related to independent reading may include the following:

• Finding your own reading spot

• Choosing books for your book box (e.g., hard, harder, and hardest books)

• Caring for books and treating them gently (e.g., no "book sandwiches" in the book box)

- Reading with your two-inch (five-centimeter) voice (i.e., the teacher places a ruler up to his or her mouth to show students how loud their voices must be to project two inches, six inches, and beyond)

- Reading with a partner (e.g., chorally from the same book, taking turns from the same book, taking turns from individual books, or "copycat" reading, in which one partner reads a section, then the other partner reads the same section)

- Exchanging books where you won't be interrupted or be able to touch anyone else

Teaching any routine takes time and patience. Allow plenty of time for modeling, demonstration, and guided practice before expecting students to function independently. Patience will pay off in a smoothly flowing independent reading program that supports children in becoming readers and lovers of books.

Home Reading Programs

A discussion of independent reading wouldn't be complete without mentioning the home—school connection. When parents are on board with the reading program, students get much needed additional reading practice and see reading as an activity that extends beyond school. They realize that even Mom and Dad read. (We hope.) A take-home reading program that extends the reading experience beyond the classroom helps children to see literacy as part of their whole lives. Some teachers select the books students take home each night to ensure that the take-home books are books from a range of options. When students select their own take-home texts, I suggest using a bookmark system to inform parents about whether each book is a "read by," "read to," or "read with" book. Before students put their chosen books away in their book bags, slip a colored bookmark into their books. A yellow bookmark labeled "Read *by* your child" indicates that the book should be at the students' independent reading level. Additional suggestions for helping the reader with difficulties are included on the bookmark. A green bookmark labeled "Read *to* your child" indicates that the book is too difficult for the student to read independently. Finally, a blue bookmark labeled "Read *with* your child" indicates that the student might be able to read or join in on parts of the book. By using the bookmarks, students are able to make their own book choices, and parents are guided not only in how to support the home reading but also in what to expect from their children as readers.

Some teachers are reluctant to initiate home reading programs because they are concerned about the books disappearing, especially when the teacher has gone to great out-of-pocket expense to supplement the classroom library. Some checks and balances, such as carding the take-home books and not permitting students to take home another book until the previous one is returned, can help minimize loss. However, it often seems

Take-Home Reading Bookmarks
- Read *to* your child.
- Read *with* your child.
- Read *by* your child.

Figure 9.3
A Sample Take-Home Book Bag

that the child who needs the reading practice most is the one least likely to return his or her books expediently. I recall one little girl who was afraid to take books home because her brothers would damage them, but she was left with nothing to read at home but grocery store flyers that arrived in the mailbox. Surely we teachers can find some way to support these little readers, even if it means replacing a few books. One alternative is to send home reproducible books from websites such as www.readinga-z.com and www .dltk-teach.com/minibooks/index.htm, and the amazing collection of websites on www .jmeacham.com/emergent.readers.htm.

Some teachers, such as Donna Koch, prepare book bags for take-home reading. These bags generally contain one or two trade books along with an artifact or hands-on activity, such as a stuffed animal, an envelope full of word cards to match to the words in the book, instructions and materials for a craft, or a game to play (see Figure 9.3). A parents' page is also included to guide them in talking with their children about the book or taking part in the enclosed activity.

There is probably no better model for a love of reading than a teacher who integrates reading and writing into every aspect of the classroom program. Few classroom activities are so simple, yet so powerful in nurturing children's literacy development.

CHAPTER 10

"I Never Knew We Could Write This Good!": Modeled, Shared, and Interactive Writing

I've always thought I was a pretty good teacher of writing. In retrospect, I think I've been a better assigner of writing. How often I've handed my students a piece of pink paper with a border of tulips and said, "Write about spring," or handed them each a journal and said, "Tell about what you did on the weekend." There's nothing wrong with either of these tasks in and of themselves, but where's the teaching? What do my students know after completing these task that they didn't know before?

Of all the tools in our instructional toolboxes, modeling may very well be the most powerful. Modeling writing for students not only demonstrates how writers think and work but also shows students that writing is an important and meaningful activity that grownups do in life as well as in school.

One great advantage to modeling is that it doesn't require a lot of costly materials. While some teachers have access to interactive whiteboards and other advanced technology, most kindergartens that I visit still rely on the lowly flip chart for modeled writing. Keep a supply of markers, scissors, and tape on hand by the chart stand to maximize instructional time.

Modeling and demonstrating the mechanics and processes of writing involves teacher–student interactions at a variety of levels of teacher support and student independence, as shown in Figure 10.1. Each level of modeling serves a range of purposes and all should be part of a well-balanced writing program.

Modeled Writing: The "Write-Aloud"

In a modeled writing experience, the teacher explains the thinking that goes on in his or her head while demonstrating what writers do. The teacher shows the students that writers think of ideas, talk about their ideas, and put those ideas on paper using letters and words (see Figure 10.2). While writing, the teacher might describe the mechanics of writing, such as stretching words to hear all the sounds or putting "spaghetti spaces between the letters and meatball spaces between the words." The teacher may point out a powerful word, show how writers read back their writing, or insert details into a piece of writing. In a modeled writing process, the students are observers, not active participants.

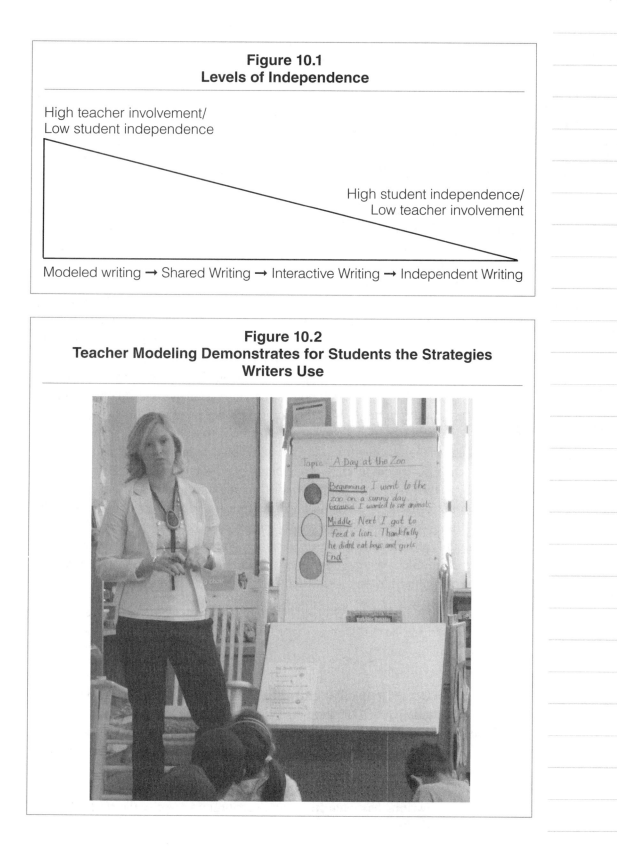

Figure 10.1
Levels of Independence

High teacher involvement/
Low student independence

High student independence/
Low teacher involvement

Modeled writing → Shared Writing → Interactive Writing → Independent Writing

Figure 10.2
Teacher Modeling Demonstrates for Students the Strategies Writers Use

What can I model?

Modeled writing may be used to teach minilessons about process, conventions, or style, including choosing a topic and adding details, stretching out words, placing punctuation marks, and asking a writing partner for help.

We teachers can use modeled writing in many different situations. Often a modeled writing minilesson introduces the writing workshop. In this case, we demonstrate a specific strategy or skill for the students to practice in their own writing. Modeled writing minilessons must be brief and focused. It's not necessary to articulate every thought that flits into our heads. Instead, we focus on one or two specific areas that we want students to learn. We can still model spaces between words, capitals at the beginnings of sentences, and the like, even if we don't explicitly draw students' attention to them through the think-aloud. It goes without saying that kindergartners have short attention spans and limited tolerance for "sitting and gitting." If a lesson goes beyond five minutes, stop and continue it the next day. It's a great model for students to see a piece of writing continued over a few days. Figure 10.3 describes a typical modeled writing lesson for a kindergarten writing workshop, focusing specifically on writing a letter.

When introducing a modeled writing minilesson, start by telling students exactly what they're going to learn and linking this new knowledge to what they already know. As Lucy Calkins (2003) suggests, try to give the strategies a catchy name that students will be able to remember and use. The instructional component of the lesson is the modeling and think-aloud part, keeping it as brief and focused as possible. Sometimes it's useful to add a guided practice component, providing students with an opportunity to try out the strategy in a situation that is designed to support practice and success, often with a partner. Finally, invite the students to try out the strategy in their own writing. This enables you to assess students' understanding and mastery of the strategy and helps guide planning for further instruction. It is this combination of explicit teaching and student accountability that transforms merely assigning writing tasks to true teaching of writing skills.

A modeled writing minilesson has three parts:

1. **Introduction:** Tell the students what they are going to learn and link the new learning to prior knowledge

2. **Instruction:** Model the new learning as part of connected text while thinking aloud

3. **Independent Application:** Invite students to try the new learning in their own writing

Determining what to model in a writing minilesson should be guided by local curriculum standards as well as assessments of students' needs. Here are some of my favorite kindergarten minilessons, more fully described in my book *Marvelous Minilessons for Teaching Beginning Writing, K–3* (Rog, 2006):

• **Keep a Topic in Your Pocket***:* Provide students with a large envelope to attach to their writing books. Demonstrate how to collect pictures (images students draw or photographs from home) that might be used for writing ideas. (See Chapter 11 for further explanation.)

• **What Is a Detail?** A detail is any piece of information about a topic. Use words like *topic* and *details*—the language of writers—when retelling a story from a read-aloud. For example, make reference to a story by saying, "What were some of the *details* Amy Rosenthal told us about Little Pea? Were any of them *surprising* details—things you didn't expect?" Recount *details* that students read, and tell students that (a) good writing has details that tell more about the topic and (b) the best writing has interesting details that might surprise the reader.

Figure 10.3
A Modeled Writing Lesson

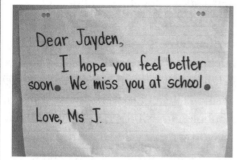

Dear Jayden,
   I hope you feel better soon. We miss you at school.

Love, Ms J.

The friendly letter may be going the way of the dinosaur, but it's still good for children to learn that a message to someone else (even an e-mail) should begin with a greeting and end with a signature. Postcards make for great message writing. Ask parents to tear the backs off old greeting cards and send the front parts to school to be used for postcard writing.

Lesson Focus: Students will understand the purpose of a letter and experiment with writing a letter that starts with a greeting and ends with a signature.

Lesson Introduction: *Boys and girls, if we want to give a message to other people, usually we can just talk to them, but if they live far away or aren't here at the moment, we can't talk to them. So we can write a letter to them. I don't mean a letter like* a, b, c. *This kind of letter is a message that we write to another person.* (If possible, refer to a past read-aloud that is written in letter format, such as *The Jolly Postman* by Janet and Allan Ahlberg, as a way to introduce the concept of letters.)

Instruction: (Model writing and thinking aloud.) *I think I will write a letter to our friend Jayden, who has been at home sick all week. A letter always starts with the word* Dear *and the person's name. So I'm going to start with* Dear Jayden.

(At this point, model moving the pencil down to the next line, under the *D* in Jayden, but don't necessarily talk about the return sweep because the lesson should not focus on too many things at one time. The lesson focus for now is just the greeting, the body, and the signature of a letter.)

I think I will say to Jayden, "I hope you feel better soon. We all miss you at school." (Write the message, word by word, but don't focus too much on individual conventions.)

Now I have to end my letter by telling him whom it's from. I could say, "Love, Ms. J." or "Your friend, Ms. J." Can you read my letter with me? See that I started with Dear *and the person's name? Then I wrote a message. Then I ended with my name so he knows who sent the letter.*

Independent Application: (Not all the students will be ready to write a letter at this point, but offer them the opportunity to try.) *Boys and girls, today in writing workshop, you might want to write a letter to someone, like a friend, or your mom, or even the teacher. Let's remember the three things we need in a letter: "Dear someone," a message, and your name.*

- **Sticky Dot Details:** Remind students that any information in a piece of writing is a detail. They are going to learn how to use sticky dots to help them remember to write more than one detail on their topic. Demonstrate and think aloud as you write two or three details on a topic and put a sticky dot at the end of each detail (much like a period).

- **Bubble Gum Writing:** Remind students that writers can write any word that they know how to say. They are going to learn how to pretend a word is a piece of bubble gum in their mouths and stretch it out to hear all the sounds. Model stretching out a word with one hand and writing a letter for every sound you hear as you stretch it. Have students practice bubble gum words on their individual whiteboards before sending them off to try it in writing workshop.

- **Capital Letter Word Sorts:** Provide students with a list of common and proper nouns. Have them sort the words into those beginning with capital letters and those beginning with lowercase letters. Together with the students, construct a rule for when a word needs a capital letter. Invite the students to add words of their own to each set; then challenge them use at least one capital letter word in their independent writing.

In other situations, modeled writing might be used to consolidate and review a number of strategies that have already been taught, such as during the morning message (see Figure 10.4). These lessons are multipurpose and multilevel; ideally, they are rich enough to provide challenges for the most capable learner, yet offer manageable learning for the less sophisticated student.

Shared Writing: Seeing Talk Written Down

We've just come back from a field trip to the local museum, and I want my students to create a collaborative report on the highlights of the excursion. I prepare the chart paper or the interactive whiteboard and invite students to contribute ideas, while I do the actual writing. This is called *shared writing*. The students are partners in determining what to say; the teacher transforms their spoken words into print.

Shared writing has its roots in the language experience approach (Ashton-Warner, 1963), in which the teacher transcribes words dictated by the students and uses these texts for instruction. Traditionally, language experience activities were designed mainly for documenting children's language and experiences. Today, shared writing can serve many purposes, including demonstrating the processes that skilled writers use. Language experience activities enable students to see their talk written down. Together, we as teachers and our students negotiate what will be written. This in itself is a powerful oral-language experience, as students learn to string together coherent ideas in interesting words and sentences. Using some form of

> Shared writing may take many forms in the kindergarten classroom, such as the following:
>
> - Daily news time
> - Classroom rules
> - Recount of a field trip
> - Group message or letter
> - Description of a science experiment
> - Collaborative report on a topic
> - Statements about the "person of the day"
> - Retelling or text innovation in response to a story

Figure 10.4
Modeled Writing During Morning Meeting

Boys and girls, today is Tuesday, and today's date is January 12, so I'm going to write the date first thing right here at the top of the page. We have an exciting thing happening today. A firefighter is coming to visit to talk to us about fire safety. Now I want to write, "The firefighter is coming today." Please count the words with me: The-space-firefighter-*space*-is-*space*-coming-space-today. *Five words and four spaces. My first word is* the *and it's one of our word wall words, so I know it in a snap:* t-h-e. *But I have to remember to start it with a capital letter because it's the first word in the sentence. I have to leave a space before I write my next word, so I'm going to hold three fingers down on the paper to mark my space. My next word is* firefighter *and that is a very big word. Can you hear the three parts? Please say it with me: "Fire-fight-er." I'd better go back and read what I've written so far: "The firefighter." Now I need to write* is coming.; *Those are two separate words—*is *and* coming. *I leave another three-finger space and write* is, *which is another one of our no-excuse words, so I know it in book writing. I leave another three-finger space and stretch* coming. *Oh, look, it has the* -ing *family at the end. One more three-finger space and our last word,* today. *You know what I notice about* today? *It's got two little words I already know—*to *and* day. *And finally, I'm going to put a little dot called a* period *to show that my sentence is done.*

Although the modeled writing lesson is not generally interactive, many teachers have found creative ways to gradually increase the level of student involvement in writing the morning message. Sometimes the leader of the day is invited to compose the message. Some teachers create a morning message puzzle, omitting words or letters from the message, inviting students to contribute the missing pieces. Kimberley Nelson, a teacher from Sarasota, Florida, USA, describes on her website (www.mrsnelsonsclass.com) Two Color Writing. Once the morning message is composed, she invites her students to contribute letters. If they guess the correct letter, she writes that letter in one color. If they don't produce the correct letter and she has to provide it, she writes it in another color. At the end, they count the letters in each color, and the students take delight in determining who "wins"!

enlarged print, write the words that students supply, modeling and demonstrating the process of writing. In Figure 10.5, the teacher used a shared writing process to record students' ideas about how to make hand prints. We often call the products of this activity *experience charts*, though they may take more technological forms than traditional charts; ideally, they should be frequently revisited for shared and independent reading as well as instruction and review of specific language features.

As an alternative to the group chart, record one idea from each student. This activity is often done individually or in small groups, rather than with the whole class. (It will

Figure 10.5
A Shared Writing Lesson About How to Make Hand Prints

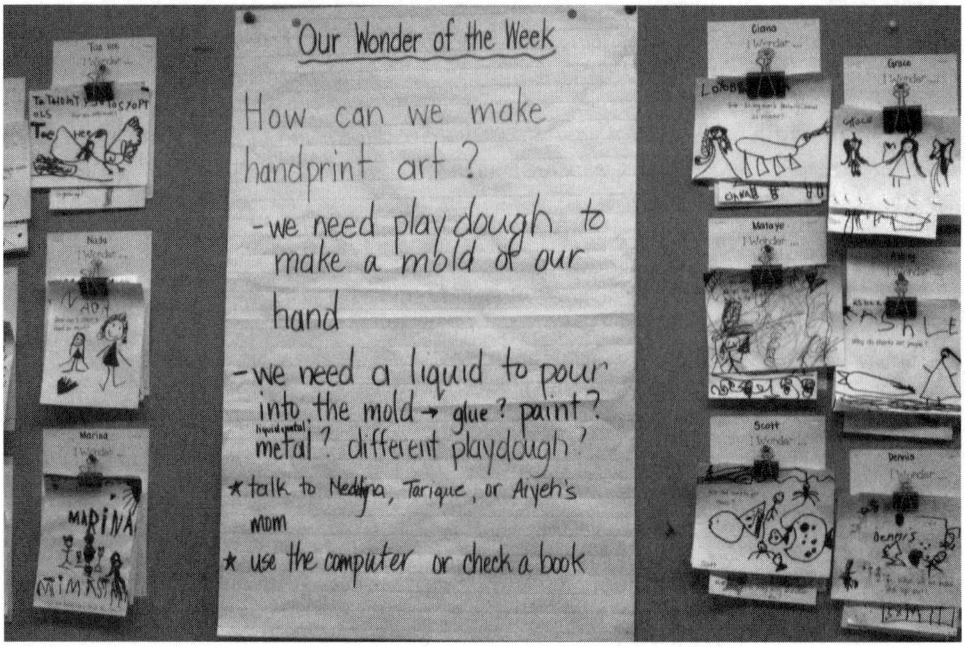

be neither interesting nor educational for students to sit through the transcription of every student response in the class.) It provides an opportunity for differentiating the language experience for each student.

Print each student's contribution on a large chart (as in Figure 10.6) and revisit the chart for students to "read" their own responses and those of others. This is a wonderful opportunity to draw students' attention to capitalized words, letter patterns, periods, and other language features. When the chart has served its purpose as a shared reading and language instruction tool, the individual student responses can be cut apart into strips. Glue each student's sentence strip onto a piece of paper and invite the student to read and illustrate it. Digital cameras make it easy to provide each student with a photograph of him- or herself to incorporate into the illustration. Depending on the developmental level of the students, you may choose to cut apart the individual words and have the student reassemble them. The illustrated sentences may then be stapled or spiral bound together in a book for the classroom library or take-home reading program.

Interactive Writing: Sharing the Pen

Interactive writing is "a dynamic literacy event in which reading and writing come together."

(McCarrier, Pinnell, & Fountas, 2000, p. 67)

In an interactive writing lesson, the teacher and students share both the composing and the writing. Heavily scaffolded by the teacher, individual students take turns "sharing the pen" to write parts of the message.

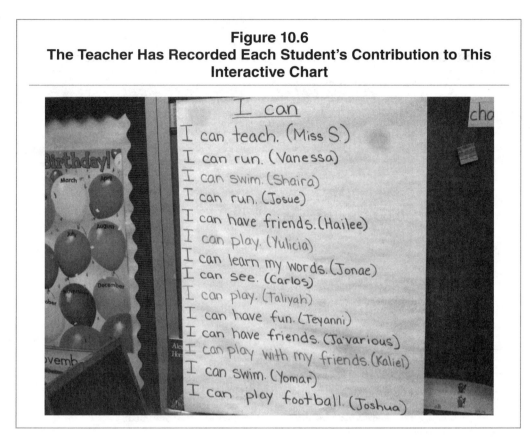

Figure 10.6
The Teacher Has Recorded Each Student's Contribution to This Interactive Chart

Together the students and teacher create a message (see Figure 10.7). The teacher selects individual students to write parts of the message, based on his or her knowledge of each student's capabilities. Some students might be invited to write the first letter of their name when it occurs; other students may be able to write some sight words, letter patterns, or more challenging words with support. This is a great time to reinforce word boundaries by having one student do the writing and another student put his or her hand after each word to remind the writer to leave a space before the next word.

I particularly like to use an interactive approach when our writing has a specific audience and purpose, such as a letter to someone as in the classroom example that follows. Because our writing is intended to be read—either by ourselves or by someone else—we want to make sure it is written in "book writing," that is, conventional spelling. I divide the page in half to create a practice part at the top and the writing part on the bottom half (see Figure 10.8). I use the top half of the page to reinforce spelling patterns, letter-sound

> During interactive writing, there are two important roles: the writer and the spacer. The spacer puts his or her hand down after each word to remind the writer to leave a space between the words.

Figure 10.7
Students "Share the Pen" in an Interactive Writing Lesson

relations, and even letter formation. The student writers also may use the top of the page to try out a word or letter before committing it to the actual writing. Here is a sample interactive writing lesson:

> *Boys and girls, we've talked about how we can write a letter to send a message to someone. Yesterday, Mr. Rogriguez came and talked to us about playground safety. I think we should write a note back to Mr. Rodriguez. What could we say to him? How does Mr. Rodriguez help us? Turn and talk to your partner about what we might say to Mr. Rodriguez in a letter. Then we'll all put our heads together to decide what the letter will say.* (Together, the students decided to write "Thank you for keeping us safe.") *Let's say those words together:* Thank-*space*-you-*space*-for-*space*-keeping-*space*-us-*space*-safe."

> *Before we can write the message, we need to start with something else. Who can remember how to start a letter to someone?* (A student answers, "Dear…".)

> *Yes, a letter starts with "Dear" and the person's name. So, first, we need to write that word* dear. *Let's listen for the beginning sound: "d–d–d". Whose name on the name wall starts with* d?

> *David, that's the first letter in your name. Would you please come up and write a capital* D *for us? Boys and girls, do you see how David makes a straight line down and a fat round*

Figure 10.8
Dividing the Paper Allows Space for Practice as Well as Writing

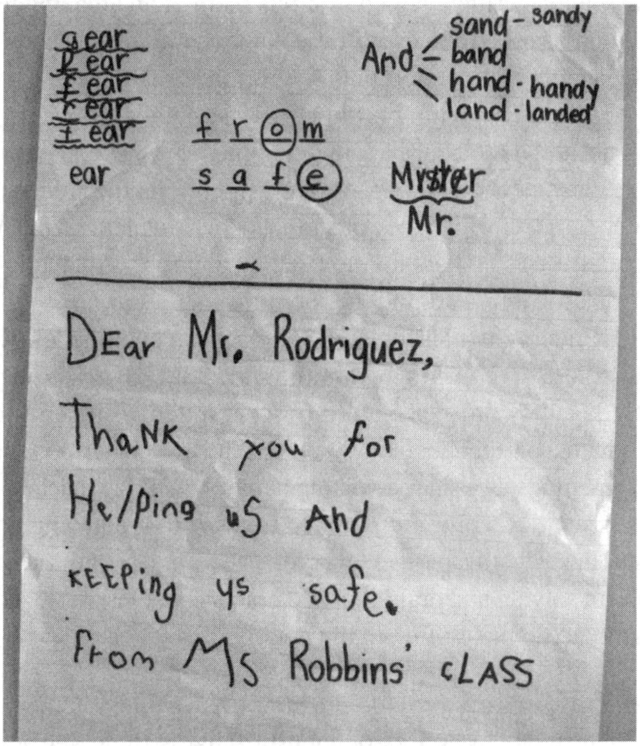

tummy on the D*? Everyone trace a capital* D *with your finger on the carpet in front of you. The word* Dear *is not anybody's name, but we make it a capital* D *because it's the very first word. Now listen for the rest of the word—*d-ear. *The rest of the word is the* -ear *family. Watch while I print the word* ear *at the top of the page. While David writes the rest of the word* Dear, *I would like the rest of you to talk to your partner about some other words that are in the* ear *family.*

Now that David has written Dear *for us, let's read the letters aloud together:* D-e-a-r. *Mr. Rodriguez has a very long name, so I'm going to write it for you, but I'd like you to say the letters with me as we write. Rashid, would you come up and be my spacer please? We need a space after* Dear *and after* Mr.

This may be all we accomplish in one day. What an important lesson for kindergartners: We don't always finish our writing in one day. Often we go back to a piece the next day and reread what we've written to add or change some details. These daily writing activities are short and may be continued over several days as long as student interest remains high. When the letter is complete, we simply cut off the practice part and put the letter part in the mail. With luck, our recipient will write back to us!

Some examples of Buzz Book prompts might include the following:

- What are some words that start with *p*?
- What are your favorite breakfast foods?
- What are some things that are round?
- Which words go together?
- What's the answer to this riddle?
- Can you tell a knock-knock joke?
- What rhymes with cat?
- What do we know about stars?
- How do you make pizza?
- How could we invite our reading buddies to our authors' party?
- What are some words related to winter?

This brief lesson has reinforced many concepts about print and language, such as capitalization, spacing, letter patterns, and punctuation. Also, as we write with our students they go back over and over again to read what they've written, which reminds them of an amazing feature of writing: it says the same thing every time someone reads it. That's a lot of teaching and learning compressed into one minilesson.

Interactive writing is slow and methodical. Because only one or two students are at the board at any one time, we teachers must make sure to engage the students on the floor. We can provide the students with individual whiteboards on which they can practice writing letters and patterns. Students might also trace letters on the floor or put on their "magic reading glasses" and look for words around the room.

Kindergarten teachers Bonnie Jackson and Shelley Vaughn describe a daily interactive writing event they call Buzz Books (www.thekcrew.net). Each day, they introduce a prompt that requires students to "buzz," that is, chat, with a partner about its solution. The text is then completed interactively (or sometimes as a shared writing activity, with the teacher scribing).

Each day's prompt is linked to a specific learning goal. Because students "buzz" with a partner, everyone gets an opportunity to participate in the problem solving and oral-language practice, not just those who will ultimately have the opportunity to do the writing in the book.

Shared and interactive writing provide the supports that enable beginning writers to stretch beyond what they can do independently. That is the essence of scaffolding—temporary instructional supports that bridge the gap between what learners can do on their own today and what they will be able to do tomorrow. Through shared and interactive writing, kindergartners learn about the forms and functions of written language and are active participants in transforming their ideas and spoken words into print.

Guided Writing

In a guided writing situation, the students do the writing, with plenty of teacher support. Students may be given a prompt or framework, may work with a partner, or may receive one-on-one teacher support. Guided writing often occurs in small groups, much like guided reading, where the teacher can offer intervention or extension to several students with common needs. This type of writing structure is common in kindergartens, enabling us teachers to work intensively with only a few students at a time on everything from generating ideas to spelling words.

The main difference between guided writing and traditional writing prompts or assignments is a focus on what the students are learning as writers, rather than on the product of the writing.

Not all guided writing needs to occur in small groups, however. Often we may use a pattern or framework to guide students in experimenting with a new text form or a certain writer's technique. For example, we might provide a framework such as the one pictured in Figure 10.9 to support children in doing procedural writing.

Literature connections can also guide student writing. The best models of good writing are the books the reader loves, and we can take advantage of these ready-made models to encourage kindergartners to stretch their writing skills. We and our students always read a text the first time for meaning and enjoyment. On subsequent readings, we can look at techniques the writer has used and then, in a guided writing situation, the students can have an opportunity to try those techniques. (An example of using a writer's technique may be found in Chapter 6, where the teacher and students used Mélanie Watt's *Scaredy Squirrel Makes a Friend* to learn and try the technique of labeled diagrams.)

Sometimes students' writing might consist of a copycat book that uses a familiar structure or concept. Many teachers have used the classic *The Important Book* by Margaret Wise Brown as a framework for a text innovation (see Figure 10.10).

Figure 10.9
How-To Writing Framework

How To _____

First, _____

Then, _____

Last, _____

Figure 10.10
A Student's "Copycat Book" Based on *The Important Book*
by Margaret Wise Brown

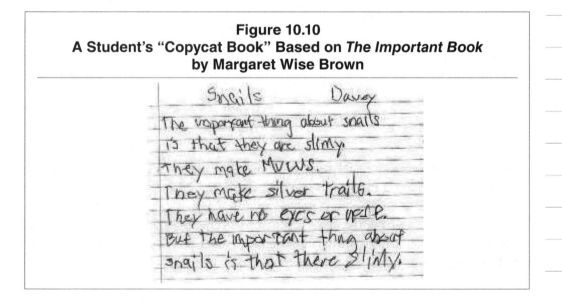

Frameworks and patterns support beginning writers as they focus on a topic, generate rich details, and use interesting words. A selection of recommended literature links and suggested writing goals may be found in Table 10.1.

Table 10.1
Literature Links for Guided Writing

Book	Suggested Writing Focus
Barrett, J. (2001). *Things that are most in the world*. New York: Atheneum.	Making comparisons
Borden, L. (1989). *Caps, hats, socks, and mittens: A book about the four seasons*. New York: Scholastic.	Repeating words for effect
Brown, L. (2006). *How to be*. New York: HarperCollins.	Writing how-to sentences
Henkes, K. (1993). *Owen*. New York: HarperCollins.	Describing sensory details, such as how something sounds, tastes, smells, and feels
Rosenthal, A.K. (2005). *Little pea*. San Francisco: Chronicle.	Generating surprising details on a topic
Ward, C. (1992). *Cookie's week*. New York: Putnam.	Writing a timeline (e.g., days of the week)
Watt, M. (2007). *Scaredy squirrel makes a friend*. Toronto, ON, Canada: Kids Can.	Creating unique text structures such as picture lists, maps, and labeled diagrams

Modeled, shared, interactive, and guided writing are supports that stretch kindergartners from where they are right now to where they can be. Mary Rubadue (2002) found through her action research on interactive writing that her students not only became more proficient writers, but they were also more willing to experiment and take risks with their writing and were more engaged and motivated to write. As one kindergartner was heard to exclaim, "I never knew we could write this good!"

CHAPTER 11

"Look What I Writ!": Building Independence With the Kindergarten Writing Workshop

In 1983, Donald Graves asked a group of kindergartners whether they could read and write. Only about 15% responded that they could read, but 85% said that they could write. For many children, writing develops more easily and naturally than reading.

Writing takes many forms in the kindergarten classroom. With our students we teachers collaboratively record class news, responses to reading, and science logs. We stock writing centers with different kinds of paper for students who choose to write stories and messages for one another. We incorporate literacy artifacts into dramatic play so students can create shopping lists, menus, or telephone messages. We invite students to record their own learning from explorations or inquiry projects. We encourage students to create environmental print such as signs or directions throughout the classroom. In each of these structures, writing is the vehicle for generating and communicating information. If we teachers want our students to become more competent and confident writers, however, we need to teach them what writers do and then give them an opportunity to practice those important skills, strategies, and habits. That is what the writing workshop does.

> "Children will only develop control over written language if they are encouraged to write frequently in a workshop atmosphere, in which they draw/write about real events in their own lives and read their work to peers in all-group share time."
>
> *(Strickland & Feeley, 2003, p. 345)*

The great strength of the writing workshop is that it combines explicit instruction and guided practice, specifically focused on learning goals in writing. Instruction is purposeful, differentiated, and developmentally appropriate. Through a balance of whole-class instruction, small-group guided practice, and individual conferences, students are supported, nudged, and scaffolded to extend their reach as writers. In many classrooms, daily journals dominate the writing program. The difference between writing workshop and journals essentially boils down to *explicit teaching* and *student accountability*. Journal writing tends to be hands off. The students do some writing, prompted or otherwise, that may or may not stretch their abilities or build their writing proficiency. Expectations are that more writing begets better writing, but there are few standards—or demands—for growth. In the writing workshop, on the other hand, students are expected to try new things, that is, to demonstrate what they have learned in the minilesson.

> Scaffolding is instructional support that bridges the gap from what students can do on their own today to what they will be able to do tomorrow.

•

Small groups are another common structure for writing in kindergarten. Students receive guided writing practice in a format not unlike guided reading, though the groups may either be needs based or heterogeneous. This structure has many benefits in that the teacher can provide more differentiated instruction and scaffolding. Unfortunately, students simply do not get as much writing time as they do in writing workshop, and many may learn to over-rely on teacher support, rather than develop independence.

I believe that the greatest strength of writing workshop is the independence and self-regulation it builds. One of the first routines I teach my students is that we are never *done with* writing workshop. From the first of the year, we work on three choices: (1) add more details to your picture, (2) add more writing, or (3) start a new piece of writing. It's never too early for students to learn to solve their own problems, ask a partner for help, or move on with something else until the teacher is available. Furthermore, the writing workshop fits well into a play- or inquiry-based curriculum because it provides the tools students need to communicate their ideas, while offering them choices of *what* and *how* they are going to write, all within the context of developmentally appropriate instruction.

> **When you're done, you've just begun!**
> You can
> • Add more details to your picture
> • Add more writing
> • Start a new piece

What Does Writing Workshop Look Like?

> **The writing workshop has three components:**
> 1. Teaching time
> 2. Writing time
> 3. Sharing time

The kindergarten writing workshop usually occupies about 30 minutes a day: 5 minutes of teaching time, 20 minutes of writing, and 5 minutes of sharing and reflection. Kindergartners should have opportunities to write every day because daily writing helps students see themselves as both readers and writers, and it supports the development of those important understandings of the forms and functions of print: Why do we write? Who will read our writing? How do different kinds of writing look different? As they experiment with letters and other symbols, students construct knowledge about letter-sound patterns that they can also apply to reading.

> **Research shows that students who participate in daily writing score higher in phonemic awareness (Snell, 2007) and spelling (Partridge, 1991) than those who write intermittently.**

Materials for writing workshop are pretty simple: something to write with and something to write on. We generally have our students use unlined paper for kindergarten; at first, many children don't have the fine motor coordination or the understanding of directionality to write on lines. A lot of students are still experimenting with separating pictures and print in their writing; even paper that's unlined on top and lined on the bottom forces this distinction too early for some. Also, it's been my experience that many students seem to be intimidated by lined paper and are more likely to fill a blank page with writing. Some teachers provide students with individual sheets for writing or provide a collection of different sizes, shapes, and colors of paper. I usually have students do most of their writing in an oversized scrapbook or drawing book such as the one pictured in Figure 11.1. Additional writing that's done on individual sheets can be inserted into the book.

Again, because of fine-motor coordination challenges, I usually prefer to give students oversized writing utensils, such as fat markers. The advantage to markers is that

Figure 11.1
An Oversized Drawing Book Serves as a Kindergartner's
Writing Book

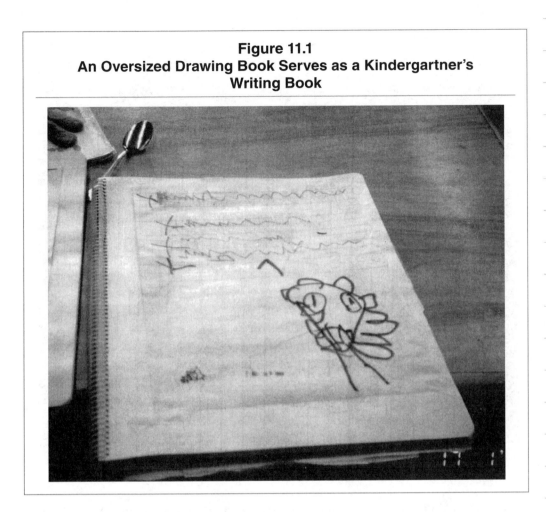

they can't be erased. I teach the students to draw a line through anything they want to change and just keep on writing. The ability to see how students have changed their minds while writing can be a valuable window into their thinking—almost a miscue analysis in writing!

Teaching Time

Writing workshop generally begins with a brief minilesson (5–10 minutes maximum, depending on the attention span of the students) that focuses on a specific learning goal (see Figure 11.2). Minilessons may focus on writing workshop routines and behaviors such as students moving on to something else while waiting for help, or they may focus on skills and strategies of writers, such as invented spelling, topics and details, or how to write a letter. The writing minilesson almost always takes some form of modeling. We gather students around us to show them, briefly and explicitly, what good writers do. The modeling may take place on an interactive whiteboard, an overhead projector, or a sheet

Figure 11.2
A Teacher Models Sentence Writing in the Writing Workshop

of chart paper, and it may or may not be interactive. Let's not feel guilty about offering short bursts of direct, explicit instruction to take advantage of very short attention spans. (See Chapter 10 for more ideas on modeling in writing instruction.) The bulk of the writing workshop should be spent on student writing, usually encouraging students to try out the tool or technique that was modeled.

Writing Time

After the minilesson, it's the students' turn to write. In kindergarten, teachers and students should always talk before writing. (Inevitably, kindergartners will also talk during and after writing!) Ask students to explain to you or to a partner what they intend to write about. Students have so many things to think about when they write—how to form letters, how to represent sounds, and how to put ideas together. If they can verbalize ideas before writing, it leaves them more mental energy to devote to getting those ideas down on paper. Only when students can articulate what they're going to write about should you encourage them to start writing. The pretelling process enables those who are ready to write to get started and provides students who struggle for ideas with an opportunity to get an idea from another writer. It also gives you a chance to provide an individual jumpstart for those who need it.

It's useful to have students sit with writing partners from the minilesson through the writing workshop. This way, they have someone to "buzz" with, to question, and to bounce ideas off during writing time. Sometimes the partnerships are random, sometimes the teacher forms the partnerships, and sometimes the students should choose their own writing partners. (A minilesson early in the year is likely to focus on modeling and practicing the behaviors of good writing partners, such as how to listen when your partner wants to read to you and how to help your partner if he or she asks.)

After students have shared their ideas with their partners, they should be encouraged to draw a picture of their story and add some "writing" (see Figure 11.3). In early

Figure 11.3
Writing Workshop Empowers Kindergarten Students to See Themselves as Readers and Writers

kindergarten, the drawing and telling parts of the writing workshop are probably more important than the print since children learn to communicate ideas through symbols.

The writing process in kindergarten basically consists of the following: (1) tell what you're going to write, (2) draw a picture, (3) do some writing, (4) print your name, and (5) stamp the date. (Of course, the use of the stamp pad entails another important procedural minilesson.) In one school I visited, students are taught to fold up the bottom of the paper, and that part will become the writing part when the picture is completed. The teachers there find that this encourages the students to include writing in the piece (see Figure 11.4). We kindergarten teachers shouldn't spend a lot of energy having students "publish" writing in kindergarten; students learn little from recopying or correcting their work, especially when they haven't yet discovered that writing says the same thing every time you read it.

Keep a Topic in Your Pocket! On rare occasions I may provide a topic or prompt, but usually I encourage students to choose their own topics for writing. Everyone writes with more commitment, voice, and engagement when writing about what matters to them,

Figure 11.4
Folding a Piece of Paper Encourages Students to Save Some of Their Page for Writing After They Finish Drawing

and kindergartners are no exception. At the beginning of the year and throughout the year, we should offer minilessons and support for finding topics, but in truth, the more frequently students write, the less difficulty they will have thinking of topics to write about.

Occasionally throughout the year, I offer minilessons and support for finding topics for writing, such as the Big Ideas Bag. The Big Ideas Bag starts as an ongoing list of potential writing topics posted on a chart in the classroom (see Figure 11.5). Each day, we work together to add a few ideas from classroom events or topics of study. When the page is filled, cut the topics into strips and put them in a large gift bag. If they are ever having trouble thinking of an idea, students can draw an idea from the Big Ideas Bag. However, in my class if students draw topics from the bag, they must write about those topics because I know that everything in that bag is a shared experience for everyone in the class.

Figure 11.5
The Big Ideas Bag Contains Writing Topics Taken From Classroom Experiences and Themes

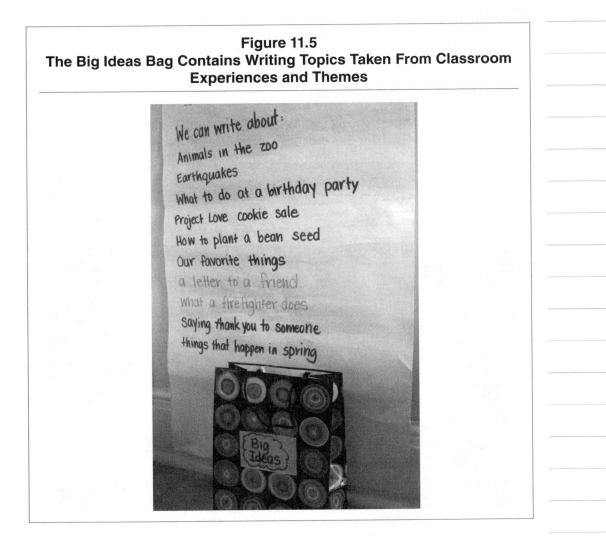

Conferring. As students write, it is our job as their teachers to circulate around the room, conferring quickly with each student as needed. I call these brief contacts *butterfly conferences* because I flit around the room and alight briefly at each student's spot to offer support, instruction, and encouragement (see Figure 11.6). These conferences enable me to differentiate instruction to meet the individual needs of my students and provide that critical just-in-time teaching for every child.

As I alight at each student's writing spot, I always start by asking the child, "Tell me what your writing says." Jennifer Jacobson (2010) suggests that asking children to tell what's happening in their pictures encourages them to generate more details. I might ask a question about the writing or offer a suggestion about a letter or word that the student has used. I want my students to know that they can always go back and add more details or change their picture or their words. I only hover by each student for a minute or two; this enables me to circulate through the class several times during the writing workshop. Table 11.1 offers suggestions for supporting students at different stages of writing development.

Even kindergartners need to know how to keep going if they're not sure how to write a word or how to move on if they finish a piece of writing. One of the first

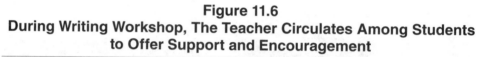

Figure 11.6
During Writing Workshop, The Teacher Circulates Among Students to Offer Support and Encouragement

routines to model and practice (and practice and practice) is what they should do when they think they're done writing. Students have three choices: (1) They can add more details to their picture, (2) they can add more writing, or (3) they can start a whole new piece. This essential routine helps build student independence and frees the teacher to work with students as needed.

Table 11.1
How to Help Children at Different Levels of Writing Development

If children are...	Then encourage them to...
still just drawing pictures	tell about their drawing and use whatever writing symbols they know
using a combination of random letters, symbols, and pictures	add details to the drawing and talk about them, and separate the writing from the drawing
writing strings of letters	tell what is happening in the story and make letter-sound connections
demonstrating left-to-right directionality and using letter-to-word correspondences (e.g., *2* for *to* or *b* for *boy*)	listen for beginning and ending sounds and make spaces between words
using beginning and ending sounds and separating words	add vowels and copy words from around the room
using invented spelling and some conventionally spelled words	write longer pieces and begin to edit

---

To Transcribe or Not To Transcribe? As I flit from one student to another, one thing I'm usually *not* doing is transcribing (or "under-writing") their writing into conventional print. Teachers differ in their attitudes toward this practice. Some like to have a record of the intent of the writing. Others believe that transcribing undermines the beginning writing process and diminishes the writers' confidence. My thinking is that I have better ways to use my instructional time that contribute more to the students' growth as readers and writers. Occasionally I will transcribe if I have a specific reason for doing so. Sometimes, for assessment or for public display, it might be useful for us to tell students that we are going to print their story in book writing as well as their own writing. Most of the time, however, emergent writing may be left to stand alone because children use it to construct their knowledge of how print is used to convey ideas.

Sharing Time

Sharing with others is an ongoing feature of any writing workshop. Before writing, students share by discussing the topic and planning what they are going to write; during writing, they share as they explore written language and collaborate to problem solve the spelling of words; and after writing, they share to celebrate what they have done. After all, people write so someone will read it. The cry, "Look what I writ!" can be heard again and again in kindergarten classrooms.

At the end of writer's workshop, the students and teacher all come together to reflect on what students have accomplished and learned as writers, and students take turns reading pieces of writing for the group. This sharing time is often called the *author's chair*, and many classes have special chairs designated for this purpose (see Figure 11.7). Providing a microphone adds a certain cachet to the sharing time and amplifies tiny voices so everyone can hear them. Sharing time is an excellent time to model and practice habits of active listening and positive response (which we call "hugs" or "stars"). (It's important to model specific compliments, such as "I loved your surprising detail about the cat jumping into the bathtub" or "That word *crinkly* is a wow

> The writing workshop structure establishes key expectations for the kindergarten classroom:
>
> • We are all writers.
>
> • We all write in different ways.
>
> • We all write about different things.
>
> • We can help each other with our writing.
>
> • We will all have a chance to share our writing.
>
> • We will all get hugs for our writing.

Figure 11.7
The Author's Chair Is an Opportunity to Share and Celebrate Student Writing

word!" When the audience is taught to listen politely and respond positively, young writers get the message that their writing has value, and they learn to see themselves as readers and writers.

Stages of Writing Development

In addition to understanding the basic structure and expectations of writing workshop in kindergarten, it's important to understand the developmental needs of kindergartners as they embark on their first writing workshop. Children arrive at the kindergarten classroom doors at many different stages in their ability to communicate their ideas in writing. At first, many children will represent their ideas only through pictures or with scribbles ("curly lines") to represent writing. Through many experiences with print and opportunities to write in the kindergarten year, most children arrive in first grade with a strong sense of the alphabet and how it works to communicate ideas.

Emergent Writers: Marks on a Page That Tell a Story

Most kindergartners are aware that pictures tell a story. Some add scribbles or even strings of random letters and letter-like symbols to their pictures. As they begin to connect print with meaning, their writing usually consists of simply labeling their pictures, such as the picture in Figure 11.8.

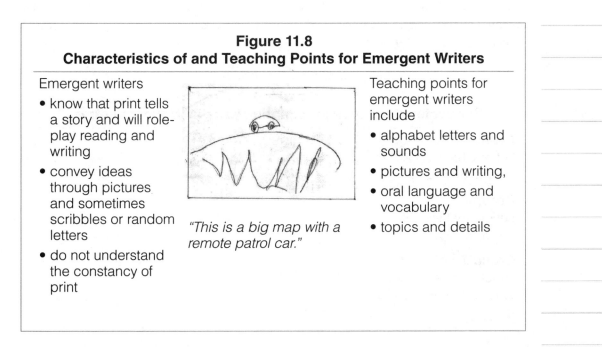

Figure 11.8
Characteristics of and Teaching Points for Emergent Writers

Emergent writers
- know that print tells a story and will role-play reading and writing
- convey ideas through pictures and sometimes scribbles or random letters
- do not understand the constancy of print

"This is a big map with a remote patrol car."

Teaching points for emergent writers include
- alphabet letters and sounds
- pictures and writing,
- oral language and vocabulary
- topics and details

Kindergarten writers are likely to put marks on a page without intending any specific meaning in advance, then decide what the marks mean when the piece is complete. For example, when observed at the writing center, five-year-old Mark was asked what he was writing. "I don't know," replied Mark, "I didn't draw the picture yet." At this stage, children realize that print symbols convey messages, but they do not yet understand that the symbols remain constant and convey the same message every time. What they "read" one day may bear no resemblance to what they read another day! Many teachers tell students that their writing is "magic" writing because they are the only "magicians" with the power to read what they wrote. At this stage, oral-language development may be even more important than the ability to connect letters and sounds (Sulzby et al., 1989). It's important to help students develop the vocabulary and language structures that they will need for writing.

> Some teachers say children's writing is "magic writing" because they are at the stage in writing where they know the functions of print but are not yet aware of sound–symbol relations. You may tell students they are magicians because they are the only ones with the magic power to read their writing, as opposed to "book writing," which anyone can read.

We also need to focus on teaching the alphabet—letter names and sounds as well as letter formation. It's been my experience that alphabet letters are effectively taught through the most important words in the children's vocabulary—their names. More information about using names to teach the alphabet may be found in Chapter 12.

Teacher modeling helps students see how the letters should look. There are many play-based activities during which students can practice letter formation, including tracing letters in sand, finger paint, and even pudding. Correct letter formation may not be a realistic goal for all children in early kindergarten, but through carefully structured experiences with print, most children learn how to construct letters that they (and others) can identify. Jan Richardson (2009) suggests that small-group instruction is the best time for letter-formation practice. Take one minute a day to have students practice the basic shapes of a letter by writing it in the air with big movements, tracing it on the table with a finger, and writing it on a board or paper, using the suggested sequence in Figure 11.9.

Figure 11.9
Suggested Sequence for Learning to Print Alphabet Letters

Group 1
Letters that start like *c*:
c, o, a, d, g, q

Group 2
Letters that start like *l*:
l, t, h, k, b, r, n, m, i, j, p

Group 3
Letters that are unique:
e, f, s, u, v, w, x, y, z

(Adapted from Richardson, 2009)

Early Writers: Connecting Letters and Sounds

Using alphabet letters in a meaningful way to represent the sounds of speech is a significant developmental milestone (see Figure 11.10). At first, young writers may represent entire words with a single initial consonant—usually the initial sound. They gradually add final sounds, such as *bk* for *book* or *lp* for *lip*. Later, medial consonants appear, followed by long and short vowels. Short vowel sounds are the most difficult for young readers to hear and to spell conventionally. Ultimately, students need to be able to represent every sound in a word with a letter or combination of letters. This ability to stretch out a word to hear all the sounds, and represent every sound with a letter, is known as *invented*, *temporary*, or *phonetic* spelling.

> Invented or temporary spelling is a powerful tool for linking phonemic awareness (the sounds in words) with phonics (the letters that represent those sounds). Research shows that writers who are encouraged to use invented spelling in early grades become better conventional spellers in later years (Clarke, 1988).

Children must be encouraged in their approximations of letter formation and spelling. This is how they construct knowledge of how the English language goes together and ultimately become confident and competent writers (Clay, 1975). I call invented spelling *bubble gum writing* because the speaker stretches the word out of his or her mouth like a piece of bubblegum and writes a letter for each sound.

Just because we teachers honor invented spelling, however, does not mean that we should ignore conventional spelling and high-frequency words. For example, I teach the word *I* on the first day of school and tell the students, "From now on, when you hear your voice say *I*, it should look like like *I*."

Once students have begun putting their words on paper, a common hurdle is moving past "one detail, now I'm done!" An important understanding for beginning writers is what a detail is. I teach the students that a *detail* is any piece of information in writing, such as *I have a dog*. Authors never stop at one detail. They use many details to tell a story. In conferences, I talk about the details in the students' pictures and how they can

---

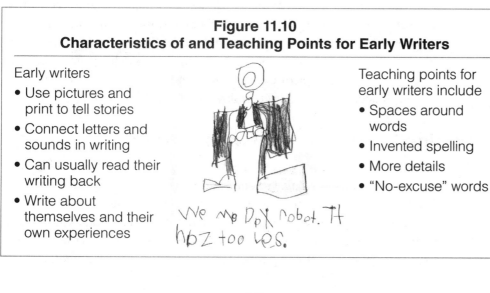

Figure 11.10
Characteristics of and Teaching Points for Early Writers

Early writers
- Use pictures and print to tell stories
- Connect letters and sounds in writing
- Can usually read their writing back
- Write about themselves and their own experiences

Teaching points for early writers include
- Spaces around words
- Invented spelling
- More details
- "No-excuse" words

137

add more details to both their pictures and their writing. I might ask, "What color is your dog? How big is he? What does he do?" Often that's all it takes to get students to put elaborative details on paper.

When students can generate several details with readable phonetic spelling, they are on their way to becoming fluent writers. Although most children go through a fairly consistent sequence of development, Sulzby and her colleagues (1989) remind us that the transition toward conventional literacy may be recursive, rather than linear: Children often revert to previous stages or may function at different stages for different writing purposes. For example, the child who is writing wonderfully creative pieces in invented spelling may suddenly discover that there is a right way to spell words and begin limiting his or her vocabulary choice to words he or she knows how to spell conventionally.

Launching the Writing Workshop

I used to think that we teachers shouldn't start kindergarten writing workshop until later in the year to provide time to establish some classroom routines and teach some literacy concepts. Inevitably, however, I had students who refused to participate, complaining that they didn't know how to write. Now I start writing workshop the first day of school. I want my students to know that writing is something we do every day, right from the first day of school. I want to hook them on writing before they figure out that they don't know how to do it! When I start writing workshop on the first day, I almost never have students who resist. As Martinez and Teale (1987) point out, "They seemed to accept the request to write as simply one more strange event in a day full of strange experiences" (p. 445).

My first minilesson of the year is usually How to Write in Kindergarten (see Figure 11.11). I gather the students together at the flipchart or interactive whiteboard and ensure that everyone has a writing partner with whom to turn and talk. I tell the students that we will be writing every day in school. I show them a book and say, "Just like in the books we read at home and at school, we will make pictures and writing that go together to tell a story. We are all writers, just like the people who make the books we read." I draw a picture and model three ways to write, as described in Figure 11.11. At the beginning of the year, I'm happy to accept any combination of letters, pictures, letter-like symbols, and even scribbles. I just want my students to get their ideas down on paper.

> Make sure every student has a writing partner. If you want them to "buzz" during the lesson, tell them, "Eye to eye, knee to knee, turn to your partner, 1,2,3."

Supporting Writers Throughout the Year

As students build their knowledge of the alphabetic principle, they need to start integrating letters and sounds into their writing. Gradually, my expectations of letter-sound connections increase. As I flit around the room, conferring with students individually, I might suggest, "*Dad* starts just like *David* on our name wall. Why don't you put a *D* right there for *Dad*?" or "When you hear your voice say '*I*' remember to write *I* in book writing." As students begin to develop a repertoire of letter-sound associations, I

Figure 11.11
A Minilesson: How to Write in Kindergarten

Introduction: Boys and girls, just like in the books we read at home and at school, we will make pictures and writing that go together to tell a story. Today you're going to learn about different ways to write in kindergarten.

Instruction: I'm going to write about what I did on my summer holidays. I went camping in the mountains! I'm going to draw a picture of the mountains, a nice stream running by, and the sun shining brightly. Here's a picture of my tent; and there's me in the tent smiling and waving. Those are all my details. Now I'm going to add some writing. I'm going to write I went camping in the mountains. In kindergarten, there are different ways to write. Sometimes we do "curly writing" that looks like this. (Teacher scribbles on the flipchart or interactive whiteboard.) Sometimes we write letters that we 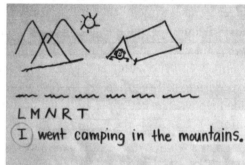 know or that we copy from around the room, and sometimes we do what's called book writing. Book writing is the kind of writing that we read in books. It looks the same for everyone. Curly writing and letter writing are kind of magic writing; only the writer can read them. But book writing is for other people to read. You probably don't know very many words in book writing right now. Maybe you know your name in book writing. But you're going to learn lots of words in book writing this year in kindergarten. And if you don't know a word in book writing, you can do curly writing. Here's a word you use all the time and you can all write in book writing: *I*.

Guided Practice: I'd like you to use your own whiteboard to practice curly writing. Next, try to write whichever alphabet letters you know. If you don't know any, copy some from around the room. Now try writing the letter *I*. Let's practice it in the air first. A straight line down, with a little line across the top and the bottom. Then let's practice by tracing the letter *I* with a finger on the floor. Got it? Now try writing it on your whiteboard.

Independent Application: Today in writing workshop, I'd like you to try a picture and some writing. You can do curly writing, letter writing, or book writing. Tell your partner what you're going to write about, and then you can get started on your picture.

encourage them to stretch out words to hear all the sounds, or do bubble gum writing. Gradually they phase out scribbles ("curly" writing) and establish the expectation that all writing will be with letters. Some experts suggest that students write a blank line for sounds that they hear but don't know how to represent (Feldgus & Cardonick, 1999). I generally encourage students to try to find a letter first and use a line only when all else fails.

Over the years, my respect for kindergarten writers has grown tremendously. I've observed that, when engaged, many children can spend 30 minutes or more on a writing task, without teacher intervention. I used to think that there must be adult support for all stages of the writing process; now, while I think that adult support is useful, I know that my students can write without constant support. I will help them with words, but they need to try those words on their own first. I use their bubble gum writing to see what they know, and I praise what they've done right: "Wow! That's a five-letter word, and you already have three of the letters. You've written most of the word in book writing already!" I can offer quick teaching at the point of need: "That *k* was a great guess for *camping*, but check on the name wall for another letter that makes a /c/ sound." If students only ever write with teacher support, they never learn to write on their own. They need to learn to self-regulate, try to solve their own problems, seek help from peers, and provide help when asked, or to move on to something else until the teacher is available. Learning those skills is the goal of writing workshop.

Final Thoughts

The writing workshop is a powerful structure that enables us teachers to offer explicit instruction to the large group, while differentiating support and expectations for indi-

viduals. Educators know that code-related instruction is best taught in the context of meaningful reading and writing (Reutzel, Oda, & Moore, 1989). David Pearson, in a 2002 interview with the National Writing Project, stated that children learn phonics and phonemic awareness "in a much more incidental, less laborious, and more natural way" through writing. He believes that phonics is more easily learned through writing than through reading because it is more transparent and more active. In a 2010 study, Cindy D'On Jones, Ray Reutzel, and Jamison Fargo found that interactive writing (described in Chapter 10) and writing workshop were effective structures in promoting phonological awareness, alphabet knowledge, and word reading. Their recommendation: Start a writing program and start it early.

Teale and Yokota (2000) remind us teachers that even 20 years ago writing in kindergarten was rare. Today we realize that when we invite children to write in their own ways, we honor their developmental stages and lay the groundwork for effective communication of ideas. Writing workshop helps young learners develop phonemic awareness, phonetic processing, sentence and story structure, understanding of genre, and critical reading and listening. And just as important, it shows students that their ideas have enough value to be preserved in written form and read by others (Figure 11.12). Few literacy experiences are more powerful than that.

Figure 11.12
Results of Writing Workshop

CHAPTER 12

Putting the "Play" Back in Word Play

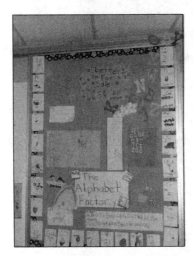

Our favorite preschooler is just starting to discover language play. At the moment, he takes great delight in coming up with rhyming names for his grandfather: What do we call Papa when he makes a mess? Sloppa! What do we call him when he cleans it up? Moppa! And while we've already begun to question our wisdom in introducing him to knock-knock jokes, we know that games like these can help to instill an interest in and love of language that will support his literacy development for a long time.

Somewhere along the line, word *play* disappeared and was replaced by word *work*. Pressures on children to be conventional readers at earlier ages and pressures on teachers to make that happen have made learning about letters and words serious business. In many kindergarten classrooms, it's more common to see students sitting at desks completing worksheets than assembling puzzles or making words from playdough letters. Surely it's time to put the play back in word play! There are many ways to fill kindergartners' literate lives with engaging, interactive, and developmentally appropriate experiences with letters and words that are both playful and purposeful.

Irene Fountas and Gay Su Pinnell (2002) suggest a word study continuum that systematically introduces concepts of print, phonological awareness, and letter awareness in prekindergarten and early kindergarten, followed by letter-sound relationships, spelling patterns, and high-frequency words in midyear and structural analysis (root words and endings, plurals, etc.) later in the year. Throughout all the primary grades, word-solving actions (strategic behaviors for analyzing unfamiliar words) are integrated into the word study program.

> "A child's name has singular importance as he embarks on learning about literacy, both for the child's management of his own learning about print and for the observant teacher trying to understand his pattern of progress."
>
> *(Clay, 1991, p. 98)*

Learning Language Concepts Through Children's Names

What's the most important word in any child's vocabulary? His or her own name, of course! For most children, their names are the first words they connect orally and in print. Their names are the first words many children learn to write. Even children who do not have the background experiences or fine motor skills to print their own names can often recognize them in print. Kindergartners' own names are the most powerful tools we as teachers have for providing systematic instruction in alphabet letters and sounds, and how those sounds are combined to form words. It's easy to create a name wall in the kindergarten classroom Find a wall space that is accessible and visible to all students and display each letter of the alphabet in uppercase and lowercase form (see Figure 12.1). This wall will be used to display the students' names, one at a time, for word work—and play. The name wall will remain in place all year, with other words added as references for the children.

Each day, appoint a different person to be the leader of the day. Post the leader's name on the name wall for that day and spell, chant, cheer, and print it with the class. I like to have students interview the leader of the day, a routine that provides important oral-language practice, particularly in asking and answering questions. I then record two or three of the responses on a sheet of 11×17 paper. Later the leader of the day can illustrate the page (see Figure 12.2) and all the pages can be bound into a class book.

Here are some routines for word play with the name of the day:

- Point to the letters one by one and call or cheer the letters in the name, pointing to each letter as it is named. In a name cheer, the teacher (or the leader him- or herself) calls out the letter and the students say it back: *"Give me a T!"* "T!" *"Give me an O!"* "O!" *"Give me an M!"* "M!" *"What do you have?"* "Tom!"

- Repeat the letters in a chant, rhythm, or even a melody. Add snapping fingers, hand-clapping or even marching to the rhythm to add some kinesthetic learning.

> Systematic instruction requires that letters and sounds be taught in a deliberate and purposeful sequence. Determine ahead of time the order in which the names will be selected, based on the most effective sequence of instruction.

Figure 12.1
A Kindergarten Name Wall

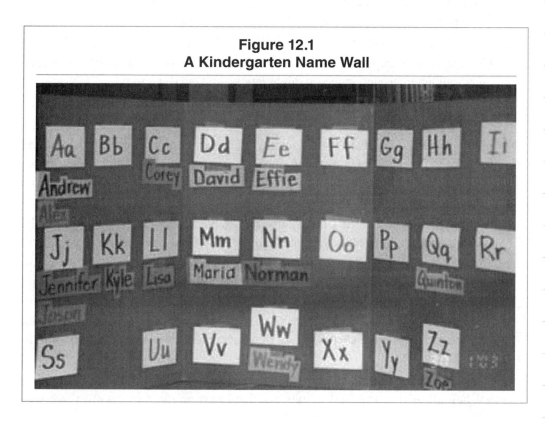

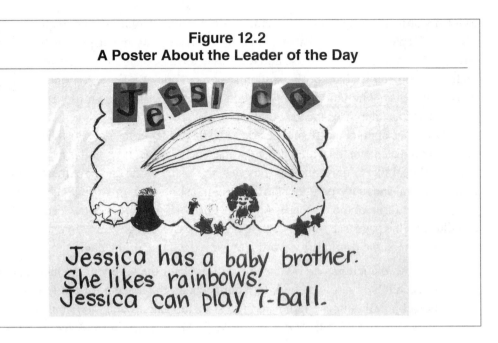

Figure 12.2
A Poster About the Leader of the Day

- Count the letters in the name. This not only reinforces the letter names (and beginning capitals) but also draws attention to the varying lengths of words. Compare the number of letters with other names. Link to numeracy by maintaining an ongoing graph of how many letters are in the names studied by the class.

- Talk about the shapes and structures of the letters in the name. Look for tall letters, tail letters, round letters, straight letters, and curved letters.

- Cut apart the letters in the name, and invite the leader to put his or her name back together.

- Talk about the sounds in the name: beginning and ending sounds, syllables, and sounds in the middle. Have students hold an imaginary rubber band in their hands and stretch their hands apart as they segment the sounds in the name. Then they can "snap" the sounds back together, saying the whole name as they clap their hands.

- Compare each new name with existing names on the word wall. Which starts the same? Ends the same? Has the same number of syllables? Has letters in common?

- Model and practice printing the first letter of the featured name. Resist the temptation to correct students' writing attempts, and do not expect conventional letter formation from the start. Remember, this is time for experimentation. Let students practice tracing the letter in the air in big motions and then tracing the letter on the table or on the carpet before they print the letter on paper or on an individual whiteboard.

- Post the name under the appropriate alphabet letter on the wall as the last routine. When all of the students' names are displayed on the name wall, there will probably be empty spaces for some letters. This is an opportunity to include other names important to the students, such as their school's, town's, or principal's name. Fill in any additional blanks with concept words such as *fish* for *F* or *house* for *H*. One word per letter is enough, though there will probably be more than one name for some letters. The point is to give students a reference point for alphabet names, symbols, and sounds.

Why choose name routines over the time-honored (but pedagogically questionable) tradition of the letter of the week? The main advantage of the name wall is that it presents the language concepts in the context of meaningful words, rather than in isolation. Second, when we introduce one name a day, we can cover the entire alphabet in a couple of months, rather than in 26 weeks as happens with one letter per week. Once the name wall is on display, we can use it to reinforce and apply letter-sound knowledge. As you draw students' attention to words, point out, "This word starts the same as *Dylan*," or "This word ends like *Sunil*." Some teachers go through the alphabet again and again with the students' last and middle names. Others use the name wall to display environmental print such as labels and wrappers from familiar products. Often the name wall is expanded later in the year to include high-frequency words (see Figure 12.3).

Figure 12.3
A Name Wall That Has Been Expanded to List High-Frequency Words

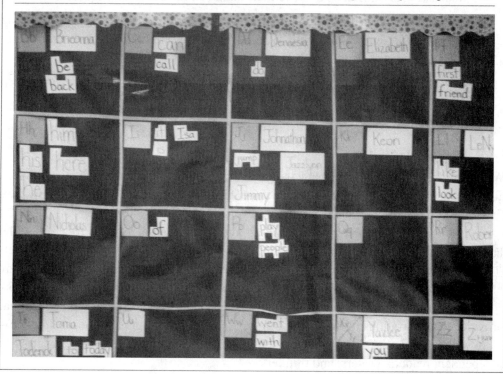

The name wall is an excellent tool for systematic introduction and reinforcement of the sounds and structures of letters and words. It also reminds students that alphabet letters are tools for reading and writing and not ends in themselves: We use letters to write our names and many other words.

The name wall routine generally takes no more than 5 or 10 minutes and is conducted with the whole class. There are also many ways to reinforce phonemic awareness and phonetic principles through students' names in small-group and independent activities. Some name games include the following:

- Adapt familiar songs to include students' names, such as "If your name begins with *B*, clap your hands," sung to the tune of "If You're Happy and You Know It."

- Use sets of name cards for various types of word sorts such as numbers of syllables, numbers of letters, names that have letters that are also in the sorter's name, or names of boys and names of girls.

- Prepare a name bag for each student, with a picture, the student's name written on a card, and a set of alphabet letters. Students can sort the letters by those in their name and those not in their name. Two students can work together to compare letters in each other's name—letters in both names and letters in neither name.

- Play Wheel of Fortune, with students trying to figure out a hidden name by guessing one letter at a time, or Bingo with students' names on the Bingo cards. Have students fill a blank card by writing their own name in the center square and asking eight friends to write their names in the remaining squares.

- Make printing practice fun by inviting students to do "rainbow writing" (tracing the letters in their names with at least three different colored markers) or print their names with cotton swabs dipped in paint.

- Have students sign in every day on an attendance sheet or daily survey (see Figure 12.4).

Letter Knowledge

When children are taught alphabet letters in the context of their names and other personally significant words, they begin to see a meaningful purpose for letters and how they fit into the puzzle of creating and decoding words.

It is important that instruction in letter recognition and naming be embedded in meaningful print use.

The problem with teaching letters in isolation, such as by reciting the alphabet or practicing one letter per week, is that the process separates letters from their purpose. When students learn letters one by one, they may become confused about letters' relations to one another and the larger task of reading (Hiebert & Raphael, 1998). A balanced literacy program that provides demonstrations of the forms and functions of print, opportunities to freely explore writing, and scaffolding to the next level of proficiency will help students grow as independent readers, writers, and thinkers.

Figure 12.4
A Daily Survey Provides Students With Practice in Writing Their Own Names

There are many playful letter-recognition activities for small-group or independent learning, limited only to the teacher's—and students'—creativity. One classroom I visited had a fish tank full of magnetic letters, and students could identify the letters they reeled in with the magnetic fishing pole. Other classes encourage students to sift out letter treasures in the sandbox or put a magnet on the nose of a stuffed dog that can then "eat" magnetic letters from a dog dish (see Figure 12.5).

Small-group reading time provides an opportunity for us teachers to differentiate instruction and practice in letter recognition and formation. Alphabet mat or alphabet arc activities include touching and naming each letter in order, naming every other letter, taking turns reading letters, reading the alphabet backward, or naming letters that come before or after a particular letter.

> Often placemats with the alphabet printed on them can be purchased very economically at a local dollar store. For a reproducible alphabet arc, see www.fcrr.org/Curriculum/pdf/GK-1/Archive/F_Final.pdf.

One group of innovative teachers guided their students in creating alphabet art books with a page for each letter that they studied. For example, students filled in the letter *D* out of *dots* with a bingo dauber, the letter *G* with *glitter glue*, and the letter *T* with scraps of *torn* paper from the recycling bin.

Figure 12.5
Stuffed Dog Is "Eating" Letters From Its Dish Using Its Magnetic Nose

Other letter games include the following:

• Treasure hunts: Hunt for letters in books or environmental print using magnifying glasses, framers (anything with a hole in it), or pointers (e.g., chopsticks, swizzle sticks, unsharpened pencils).

• Matching games: Match uppercase and lowercase letters; letters in different fonts, colors, and sizes or letters to word cards or an alphabet mat.

• Letter bingo: Print bingo cards with alphabet letters in a variety of fonts; students mark the letter that is called. They may even use plastic letters or letter cards as the markers. Players take turns rolling or drawing alphabet dice and calling out the letter for others to mark. (Thirty-sided alphabet dice—some sides are wild—may be purchased from various teacher supply outlets.)

• Letter building: Use playdough (see Figure 12.6), modeling clay, or plasticine to create letters by rolling out "snakes" to form into letters or using letter-shaped cookie cutters.

• Tracing letters: Trace letter shapes with fingers in well-sealed zipper bags containing shaving cream or hair gel.

Figure 12.6
A Kindergartner Builds Letters From Playdough

• Kinesthetic activities: Create a twister-type game board made from a shower curtain liner ruled off into a square for each letter. Students must step (or put their hand, finger, knee, elbow, etc.) on designated letters as they are called or drawn from a pile.

The Alphabetic Principle: Connecting Letters and Sounds

Children can learn the sounds of the letters at the same time that they learn the letter names. After all, 22 of the 26 letters in the English alphabet have their sounds in their names. The relation between the letters and the sounds they represent is known as the *alphabetic principle*. Knowing the relation between the sounds in words (phonemic awareness) and the symbols on the page (phonics) is an important step in children's reading development.

In its meta-analysis of research on essential components of reading instruction, the NRP (NICHD, 2000) concluded that explicit and systematic instruction in phonics is critical for beginning reading. According to the NRP, kindergartners who receive systematic beginning phonics instruction decode better, spell better, and comprehend better than children who receive incidental phonics or no phonics instruction at all. However, the NRP report found that no single approach to systematic phonics instruction was advantageous over any other. There are important messages here for teachers. Some people have interpreted the NRP recommendation as an endorsement of commercial phonics programs. Although commercial programs can offer tools such as suggested sequences of instruction or practice activities, they are just resources. No publisher knows students the way we teachers do. It is our job as teachers to use assessment to guide instruction that meets students' unique needs, rather than follow a one-size-fits-all approach.

> It is our job as teachers to differentiate instruction according to the needs and skills of the student, rather than following a "one-size-fits-all" approach.

In addition to systematic, explicit teaching, many purposeful but playful activities may be used with individuals or small groups of students to support, reinforce, and apply letter-sound understandings. Sorting activities involve grouping pictures, objects, or words according to common elements such as initial sound, final sound, vowel sounds, or rhymes. In Chapter 5, I describe one of my favorite ways to help children understand initial, medial, and final sounds by making an analogy to the engine, freight cars, and caboose of a train (see Figure 5.2). We teachers can use the same analogy to work with the initial, final, and medial letters in a word.

Many different sets of letter-sound picture cards may be found using an Internet search, and free clip art makes it easy for us to create our own. Traditional card games such as Snap, Concentration, or Go Fish may be adapted for use with letter-sound pictures. However, many kindergartners are not ready for rules-based games and may come up with their own activities that are likely to be just as effective for letter-sound practice.

Letter Patterns

We teachers will also want to introduce kindergartners to letter patterns such as consonant blends, digraphs, and word families or rimes. A rime consists of a vowel and the letters that follow it in a syllable, such as *-ill* or *-ake*. The *onset* is the phoneme at the beginning of the rhyme, such as the *b* in *bill* or the *sh* in *shake*. Learning these familiar patterns opens the doors to a wealth of words for reading and writing. In addition, introducing vowel sounds through rimes is far more consistent than by the traditional "long" and "short" patterns. I tell students that what vowels say often depends on "whom they're hanging out with." For example, a short *a* can have a variety of sound interpretations, but the /a/ sound pretty much always sounds the same when it's hanging out with *ck*.

> Over 500 primary words may be generated from the following 37 basic rimes:
>
> | | | |
> |------|------|------|
> | ack | aw | ink |
> | ain | ay | ip |
> | ake | eat | it |
> | ale | ell | ock |
> | all | est | oke |
> | ame | ice | old |
> | an | ick | op |
> | ank | ide | ore |
> | ap | ight | ot |
> | ash | ill | uck |
> | at | in | ug |
> | ate | ing | ump |
> | | | unk |

When I introduce a new word family, my students and I create a word family "house" (see the *all* family in Figure 12.7). I put the rime in the "attic," and, together, we brainstorm a few words that start with that rime. We don't need to generate every word in the world; we list six to eight words that will help us remember the rime. The advantage of the house metaphor is that if students suggest a word that has the same sound but a different spelling, as in *crawl,* I can say, "It's in the neighborhood, but it's not in the family."

Figure 12.7
Word Family Houses

Of course, rimes aren't the only letter patterns that students need for reading and writing. Instruction in consonant blends (e.g., *tr, bl*) digraphs (e.g., *sh, th*), and vowel combinations (e.g., *ea, oi*) will also be part of the word study curriculum. The Making Words strategy developed by Patricia Cunningham (1991) is a systematic approach to word study that guides students to manipulate letters and letter patterns to form words. Starting with a group of letters like *s , n, o,* and *w,* children might be instructed to make *on, no, so, sow,* and *now.* Then they're given the challenge of coming up with one word that uses all the letters. An important component of this routine is to sort the words in various ways, then come up with other words that might fit the patterns. For example, students might group *sow* and *now,* then add *wow* and *tow* to the group. This activity provides an opportunity to talk about different pronunciations of the *ow* diphthong as well as multiple meanings and pronunciations for *sow.*

> The Florida Center for Reading Research website (www.fcrr .org) has many excellent ideas for phonics games, center activities, and reproducibles, including onset-rime sliders. Students use the sliders to match initial sounds with word families, and then they complete a T-chart of the words they created, dividing them into real words and nonsense words.

High-Frequency Words

Ninety percent of the reading people do, even as adults, is made up of only 5,000 words (LaBerge & Samuels, 1974). No wonder they're called high frequency words! Of these, the first 25 are mostly conjunctions (e.g., *and, so*), prepositions (e.g., *on, in, up*),

25 High-Frequency Words for Kindergarten		
a	am	and
at	be	can
go	he	I
in	is	it
me	my	no
on	see	so
the	to	up
we	went	yes
you		

verbs of being (e.g., *is*, *am*), and articles (e.g., *the*, *a*)—the "glue" words that hold writing together. Whether they're called *snap words* (because we have to be able to read and write them in a snap), *popcorn words* (because they keep popping up everywhere), or simply *sight words*, these are the words that readers need to access automatically for fluent reading and writing. What makes these words particularly difficult is that most of them don't follow regular letter-sound patterns and most defy definition. They just have to be internalized.

Kindergartners are expected to develop a small repertoire of these most common words, and by the end of first grade they will have mastered at least 100 high-frequency words. To the best of my knowledge, there is no specific research on exactly how many words kindergartners should have in their sight word repertoire, but, as Donna Scanlon and her colleagues point out, "Because knowledge of high-frequency words provides children with so much access to reading materials, and allows them to be strategic in learning new words, setting higher expectations for sight word knowledge is probably in the children's best interests" (Scanlon, Anderson, & Sweeney, 2010, p. 228).

Ideally, high-frequency words are harvested from shared reading and writing experiences, so students can see the words both in context and in isolation. We teachers also should use different modes of learning—visual, auditory, and kinesthetic—to reinforce each word. Students might become reading detectives with magnifying glasses to hunt for the word in connected text or read around the room to find it in environmental print. They might spell the word orally, chanting it (with finger snaps or hand claps), cheering it ("Give me a *C*!"), and even singing it (such as spelling *and* to the tune of "Three Blind Mice"). They can perform actions such as "bowling" each letter, cheering the whole word as they get a "strike" at the end, or "swinging at" each letter, with a "home run" as they say the whole word at the end. Finally, they can print the word, tracing it in the air, on the floor, or even on a partner's back before putting marks on the page.

In many kindergarten classrooms, high-frequency words are displayed on a name wall (often the same wall that was used for the alphabet name wall at the beginning of the year) to be reviewed, reinforced, and revisited over and over again as a resource for reading and writing. We teach only a couple of words each week to ensure that students master the words before we add more. There are many creative ways to reinforce high-frequency words:

• Shower curtain games: Divide a shower curtain with a ruler and marker into large squares, with a high-frequency word written on each square (see Figure 12.8). Students may walk, hop, or skip along the squares, reading the words as they step on them, or they can do a bean bag toss and read the word the bean bag lands on. Students like to play "musical words" and march on the squares to music with a clipboard in their hands. When the music stops, they must read or write the word they are standing on. It's also possible to create a variation of Twister in which players are instructed to put a particular foot or hand on a given word.

Figure 12.8
A Shower Curtain Used for a High-Frequency Word Game

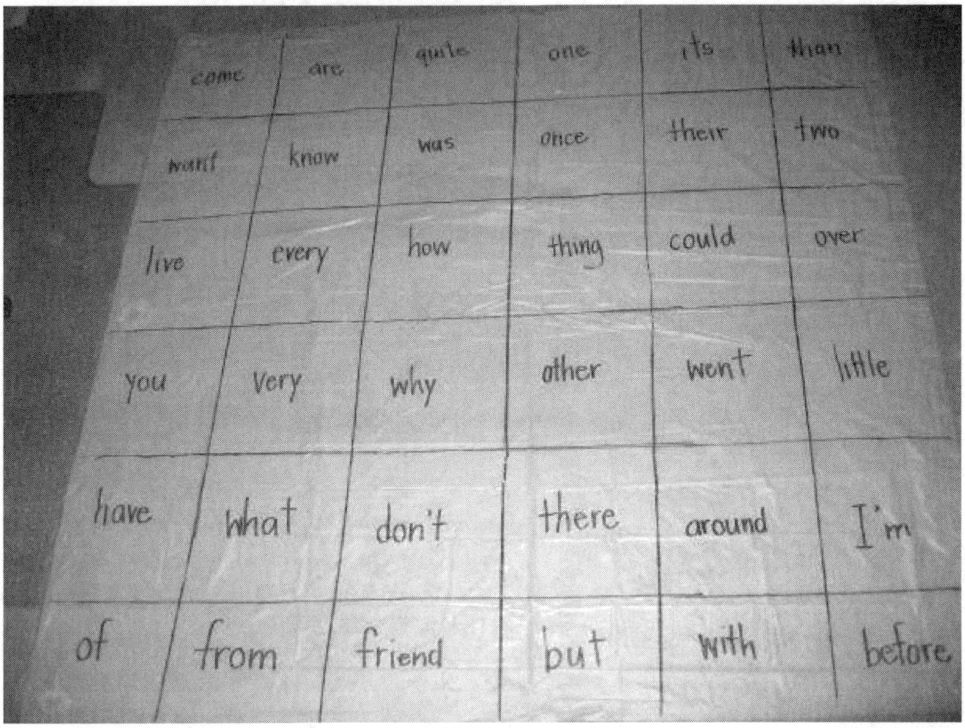

come	are	quite	one	its	than
want	know	was	once	their	two
live	every	how	thing	could	over
you	very	why	other	won't	little
have	what	don't	there	around	I'm
of	from	friend	but	with	before

- Sight word tally: Give students a marker and a page from a magazine. Given two sight words, they must highlight each time they find the words on the page and keep a tally of which word "wins" (appears more frequently on the page). It doesn't matter that the students can't read the text; the point of the exercise is to practice automatic word recognition.

- X-ray eyes (Southall, 2009): Remove letters from a known word and teach students to "see and say" the missing letters. Write a word and chant the letters with the students. Erase one letter at a time and invite students to put on their X-ray eyes (forming circles around their eyes with their thumbs and forefingers) to visualize the whole word and spell all the letters in sequence until the entire word has been erased. Repeat the game with students selecting and erasing letters in the word.

- Read it, make it, write it: Provide a three-column chart such as in the center activity pictured in Figure 12.9. Have students read each word in the first column, build it with magnetic letters in the second column, and then write it in the third column. As an alternative, students can use a stamp pad to stamp the letters on paper.

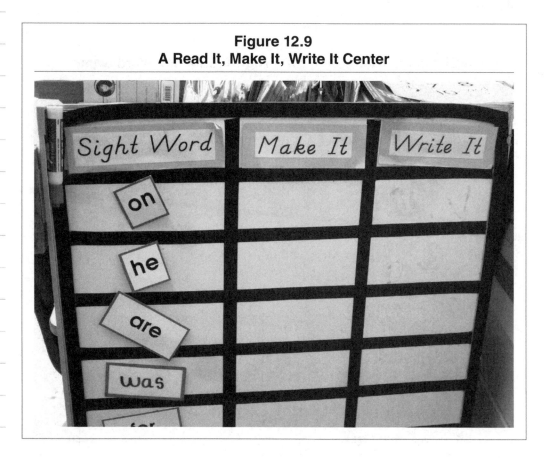

Figure 12.9
A Read It, Make It, Write It Center

Integrating Word Play Into Every Part of the Literacy Block

Understanding that words are made up of sounds (phonological awareness) and that written letters correspond to spoken sounds (phonics) are critical concepts for beginning readers. However, if phonics instruction is to be truly effective in developing independent readers, it must be embedded in a comprehensive reading and language arts program (IRA, 1997).

We teachers should reinforce concepts of print and elements of language all day long in every component of the balanced literacy program. When students listen to stories read aloud, they expand their vocabularies, background experiences, and repertoire of language structures. When they participate in shared reading and writing activities, they learn that what they see and what they write matches what they say. As students take up the pen in interactive or independent writing, they construct and apply knowledge about how letters go together to make words, sentences, and stories.

> Effective balanced literacy instruction includes systematic word study taught in the context of authentic reading and writing experiences.
>
> *(IRA, 1997)*

Integrating Language Play Into Read-Aloud Time

The read-aloud is a wonderful time to introduce interesting words and combinations of words. Alphabet books are great tools for reinforcing letter names and initial consonant sounds as stuudents learn to connect familiar objects and pictures to alphabet letters and sounds. The popular Miss Bindergarten series by Joseph Slate combines alphabetized names with rhyming text, and I've yet to meet a boy who isn't enamored with the alphabetical list of items collected in the garbage truck's hopper in *I Stink!* by Kate and Jim McMullan. Look for books with strong illustrations, text that flows naturally, and concepts that extend the reach of the children, as in the following examples:

- Books like *From Acorn to Zoo* by Satoshi Kitamura invite children to hunt for a variety of items beginning with each letter.

- *Eating the Alphabet* by Louise Ehlert, *The Wildlife ABC: A Nature Alphabet* by Jan Thornhill, and *The Icky Bug Alphabet Book* by Jerry Palotta are examples of titles that can be integrated with themes and content-area studies, introducing new concepts and vocabulary as well as reinforcing alphabet letters and sounds.

- Multicultural titles such as *T Is for Tortilla: A Southwestern Alphabet Book* by Jody Alpers or *D Is for Drum: A Native American Alphabet* by Michael and Debbie Shoulders honor the life experiences of some children and expand the knowledge of others.

> Check out www.kindergarten-tips-and-skill-lessons.com/alphabet-books.html for a comprehensive list of alphabet trade books.

Rhyming text can also have great appeal for kindergartners and help to draw their attention to the rhythms of language. The beginning reading books by Dr. Seuss have been supporting children's literacy for five decades, with ridiculous rhymes and rollicking rhythms that appeal to readers of all ages. We need to be careful with rhyming text, however. For every book with musical, natural text, there is one with contrived syntax ("My breakfast I ate") or rhymes that don't really rhyme (e.g., *crack* and *trap*). Look for books with strong rhythm, rich language, interesting concepts and text features, and rhymes that actually rhyme.

Integrating Language Play Into Shared Reading Time

Language concepts are an integral aspect of the shared reading experience. We always read aloud the poem, chart, or story several times with our students for meaning first, before isolating phrases, words, and letters. Once students are familiar with the story line, we can invite them to focus on language, using various pointers to track words one at a time while reading. Students can use any object with a hole in it as a frame to isolate words. They can use highlighting tape, waxed string, or highlighters to mark beginning and ending sounds, letter patterns, rhyming words, "words we know," and even punctuation.

> Show What You Know is a game that invites individual students to take turns pointing out any features of language that they notice in a piece of shared text. Some students may point out familiar letters or letter combinations; others may recognize actual words. They also may note punctuation marks, capitals, and other text features.

During shared reading lessons (Figure 12.10), we need to explicitly point out where to start reading, where students should sweep their eyes from the end of one line to the beginning of the next, and where words begin and end. Using our fingers to frame words, we can say, "Space to space, there's a word." Somehow addressing the spaces as entities, rather than just places without words, helps some students grasp the concept of word boundaries.

Figure 12.10
Kindergartners Can Hunt for Words and Letters in a Shared Reading Text

Integrating Language Play Into Writing Instruction

Invented, temporary, or phonetic spelling is a critical practice for beginning writers, and teachers must supported it in the classroom. This is how children develop hypotheses about the way language goes together, then test and adjust those hypotheses based on subsequent experience (Clay, 1975).

Modeled writing provides an excellent opportunity to stress letter-sound relations, phonetic patterns, and unique spellings of words. As we teachers model the transfer of spoken language into print, we are showing students how to listen for sounds and represent those sounds on paper. We teach students to put "spaghetti spaces" between letters and "meatball spaces" between words. Invented spelling is one of the most important tools for reinforcing both phonics and phonemic awareness. In Chapter 11, I discuss bubble gum writing, which teaches students to stretch words out of their mouths like bubble gum, writing a letter for every sound they hear.

We can also model how to use the resources around them to find words for writing by saying, "I can find the word *love* right up on our word wall" or "If I want to write a happy birthday note to Andrew, I can find his name right here on the class chart." Transferring words from a wall to the paper requires a level of hand–eye coordination beyond the scope of many kindergartners. Writing the words on magnetic tiles enables students to bring the words to their desks to make a closer transfer. If the location of the word wall makes it difficult for students to get close access to the words, show the students a multimodal strategy such as the say it, trace it, and take a mental picture of it routine described in Figure 12.11.

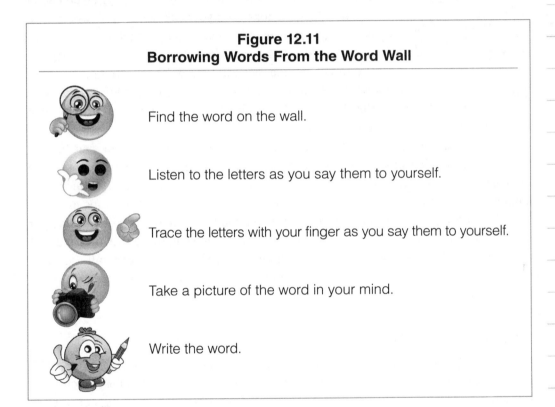

Figure 12.11
Borrowing Words From the Word Wall

Find the word on the wall.

Listen to the letters as you say them to yourself.

Trace the letters with your finger as you say them to yourself.

Take a picture of the word in your mind.

Write the word.

Language play should be just that—play. It should be fast paced and fun, with the goal of developing both students' knowledge and their motivation to take an interest in how language goes together. When we integrate language play into all aspects of literacy learning, we demonstrate to our students that language is both meaningful and authentic as we encourage the skill and will for reading that is essential to building students' foundations of literacy.

CHAPTER 13

Honoring Diversity in the Classroom

When I walked into the kindergarten classroom of my neighborhood school not long ago, I was welcomed by Yazamin, who greeted me in English and her native Farsi. Yazamin and her mother and sister are recent immigrants from Iran; they haven't seen Yazamin's father for over a year and don't know whether he is alive or not. Alejandro doesn't have a mother, but he does have two fathers; he was adopted as a baby from an orphanage in Guatemala. Blonde-haired, blue-eyed Anika is here from Sweden for two years while her father is a visiting professor at a local university. When Benny first came to the class from China, his teachers couldn't get him to say a word; now they can't get him to stop talking.

Today's kindergartens have a more diverse range of students than ever before. Some have had rich exposures to print and background experiences that make them ripe for learning to read. Others arrive at school with few literacy experiences in their own language or any other. Some speak only a language other than English, some are quite fluently multilingual, and some struggle with both the language of their home and their school. Often these are children whose culture is different from the dominant culture of their schools. Many are living in poverty. These children bring a range of cultural experiences, family traditions, and ways of knowing that make our school lives much richer but also much more challenging. We must reach and teach them all.

Children at Risk

Unfortunately, multicultural children are at greater statistical risk of having trouble with literacy. Kathryn Au (2000) has identified three factors that have an impact on children from diverse backgrounds: (1) ethnicity (the national or ethnic origin of one's ancestors), (2) class or socioeconomic status, and (3) the language or dialect spoken in the home. Note that Au did not suggest that these children learn differently from other children, only that their ways of knowing are different.

In North American societies, we tend to associate intelligence with verbal ability and richness of experience. As a result, the child who is verbal and articulate, who has had many experiences with print, and whose self-confidence has been nurtured by a safe and secure home is frequently identified as gifted. On the other hand, we may overlook the gifts of the child who did not have the benefit of intellectual and verbal stimulation before school, or who may speak a

> It is unfair and inappropriate to correlate lack of experience with lack of intelligence.

language other than English. We may label these students as "weak" when their only weakness has been a lack of experience with the English language and print. It hardly needs to be said that it is unfair and inappropriate to correlate lack of experience with lack of intelligence.

Some researchers predict that by the year 2025, 49% of the students in U.S. schools will be children of color (Smolkin, 2000), yet the majority of teachers are white and middle class. Because the cultural make-up of the teaching profession has not caught up with the diversity of students, there is often a disconnect between what multicultural learners bring to the classroom and what their Anglo teachers know and understand. This has led to what Festus Obiakor (2006) calls "misidentification, misassessment, miscategorization, misplacement, and misinstruction or misintervention" (p. 149).

Different Ways of Knowing

All children come to school imbued in the habits of their family, sometimes in the traditions of a particular country, and often in the rituals of a particular religion. Cultural diversity has particular implications for literacy instruction, affecting the way children interact with print and what they know about story. As Shirley Brice Heath (1983) showed us educators long ago, children from middle-class homes general succeed more easily in school because their ways of knowing and their literacy practices tend to match those of the school. However, all children come to school with "cultural capital"; that is, a set of values and experiences based on their family lives. We must recognize and honor these ways of knowing as we plan instruction to meet the needs of all students. On the other hand, we cannot assume that all children from a particular ethnic group will be the same in what they know, how they learn, and what they need.

> We cannot assume that all children from a particular ethnic group will be the same in what they know, how they learn, and what they need.

Robert Slocumb and Ruby Payne's (2000) research on cultures of poverty tells us that language patterns vary, not just by nationality but also by socioeconomic level. Even children whose first language is English may use nonstandard dialects that interfere with their ability to translate conventional letter-sound correspondences. Susan Neuman and Donna Celano (2001) also found that children in impoverished neighborhoods had less access to print, not just in their homes but also in their neighborhoods. Public signs were scarcer than in middle-class communities, contained less print, and were frequently obliterated by graffiti.

Children from middle-class backgrounds are accustomed to hearing the formal language structures of school used in their homes. In homes of a lower socioeconomic level, speech tends to be of casual register. For example, while children in a professional family might be asked, "Would you please pick up the fork you dropped?" children of poverty might be more likely to hear, "Pick 'at up." Within the culture of poverty, language is often sparse, informal, and functional. Because they are unfamiliar with formal registers of oral language, these children have more difficulty with written language as

> "The inability to use formal register places the students from poverty in an oral and written world that they don't understand."
>
> *(Slocumb & Payne, 2000, p. 59)*

well as spoken directions. And because they don't understand, they may get frustrated and behave inappropriately. Similarly, we teachers might get frustrated because students just "don't get it," in spite of repeated instructions.

In the same way, children of diverse cultures may have different models of using written language. Yazamin's mother reads story books to her in Farsi, reading from right to left and bottom to top. Benny's parents and grandparents use their limited English for

filling out forms and checks and performing other functional tasks, but they use only Mandarin newspapers for recreational reading. Dakota has never seen her grandmother pick up a book or a newspaper, but she enjoys listening to her grandmother's traditional tales and stories of when she was a young girl.

Even the words "Once upon a time" do not mean the same thing to everyone. One of the ways we may penalize children of nondominant cultures is in our heavy use of the time-linear story as a literacy tool. For example, some Asian cultures start with the middle of the story, then move to the beginning and the end. In the oral tradition of many African American homes, storytelling begins at the part that may have the most emotional appeal to the audience and ends with observations about the characters and their motives (Slocumb & Payne, 2000). We must remember that our sense of story is just a cultural convention.

Honoring Diversity

We expect our students to show respect for teachers and other adults, the school, and the world around them, but respect is reciprocal. Perhaps the best way to show respect for our students' cultural backgrounds is by taking the time to learn about where they come from, how they live, and how they see the world. This understanding must always involve reaching out on our part because the parents we most need to meet are those who are least likely to come walking into our classrooms. Many parents are intimidated by attending school events. Self-consciousness about language proficiency, negative memories of their own school experiences, and worry about what they might hear about their children all contribute to their discomfort. It is important to involve parents first in events that are social and nonthreatening. When schools invite the community to turkey suppers or pancake breakfasts, parents are more likely to feel comfortable attending more academic events such as assemblies and parent–teacher conferences. Parents who feel welcome in the school are more supportive of its programs and more inclined to collaborate with teachers in their children's education.

There are many ways in which schools have endeavored to make all parents feel part of the school community:

- Inviting parents into classrooms to share their knowledge and expertise, whether of culture, tradition, work, or talents
- Organizing festive events that welcome the entire neighborhood, not just the school community, with food and celebration

- Offering childcare for preschoolers so parents can attend parent–teacher conferences and other academic events

- Making home visits and sending notes to children at home

- Keeping the lines of communication open with praise and compliments as well as concerns and problems with the students

- Hiring (or finding volunteer) community workers whose role it is to liaise with cultural groups in their own languages to explain school programs, translate printed materials, and raise parents' concerns at the school

- Creating parenting centers where parents can bring preschoolers to play, network with other parents, and learn to speak English

- Making translators available for school assemblies and other events and printing portions of the school newsletter in non-English languages

- Establishing predictable routines such as sending home all printed information in a "Friday package" so parents know when to expect communication and can have it all translated at once, if necessary

What Children Need

We know that children who are culturally, linguistically, and socioeconomically diverse are at greater risk of struggling in school, especially with literacy. We know that they are over-represented in special education (Obiakor, 2006). Fortunately, we also know more than ever about best practices in literacy instruction for our neediest students.

There used to be a common misconception that children with limited experience with print need more systematic, direct instruction in skill development (Allington & Cunningham, 1997). All too often, educators fell into the trap of assuming that children at risk need more "skill and drill" and relegated them to fill-in-the-blanks and other low-level thinking activities. In her dissertation, Duke found that first-grade children in schools at a low socioeconomic level were offered quite different print environments than their peers in affluent districts. These children had fewer opportunities to interact with print, engage in writing, and read connected text; instead they spent more time engaged in activities such as copying, taking dictation, and completing worksheets (Duke, 2000b). As a result, the literacy disadvantage with which these children began was exacerbated by a lack of opportunities for engaging with print and developing positive attitudes toward reading and writing. Meanwhile, their more advantaged peers spent more time engaged in authentic reading experiences, perpetuating what Stanovich (1994) calls "the Matthew effect" (p. 281); in other words, the rich get richer and the poor get poorer.

Allington and Cunningham (1997) assert that these children of poverty need, more than any others, a "print-rich, story-rich, book-rich" classroom experience (p. 209). These are the children who depend on school to become literate. They need daily opportunities and large blocks of time to read and write (Au, 2000; Strickland, 2000). They need exposure to many types and genres of books to develop the vocabulary and experiential base that has been lacking in their preschool experiences. They need to be engaged in meaningful and motivational literacy activities that help them develop positive attitudes toward reading.

They also need purposeful and explicit instruction—in phonological awareness, alphabet letters and sounds, concepts of print, and comprehension strategies, all applied in the context of real reading and writing. They need opportunities to talk, work, and problem solve with others. They need teachers who constantly monitor their progress and adjust instruction accordingly. In other words, they need the same good instruction that all children should receive, but they need it even more.

Implementing effective instructional practices in the kindergarten classroom will be enough for most students to take their first steps on the road to literacy. For the small percentage of students who do not experience success, special interventions and adaptations may be necessary. These interventions should be (a) based on assessed needs, rather than a commercial program; (b) take place with individuals and in small groups, rather than whole-class instruction; and (c) supplement the classroom program, rather than replace it (Allington & Cunningham, 1997). Models such as Response to Intervention (RTI) engage a range of instructional supports in the school to provide a systematic and coherent system that is guided by assessment to help all students achieve.

> "I believe that the success of children of diverse backgrounds in learning to read and write in school depends on classroom teachers...who have the expertise to develop literacy curricula around and for their students and who can embrace the diversity among learners."
>
> *(Au, 2000, p. 45)*

If we as teachers set challenging but achievable learning goals for our students and consistently monitor their progress towards those goals, we can plan instruction that takes every student to higher and higher levels of literacy.

Good teachers know that there is no single method or approach that will be effective for all students. They have a repertoire of strategies for assessing student progress, implementing a balanced program of instruction, and providing interventions as necessary to take all students to higher levels of development. Ultimately, it is the teacher who makes the difference for students.

I can think of no greater challenge—or reward—than this. Occasionally, I run into students I taught years ago. They are teachers and dentists, athletes and musicians, moms and dads. I am honored to think that I had a role in their journey from the kindergarten explorers and early readers of yesterday to the literate citizens of today.

In 20 years, when today's standards and initiatives are dim memories, our students will be fully-grown testimony to the art and skill we brought to our classrooms when they were young. We know that every year in school is important, but surely no single year is more vital than kindergarten. The routines we establish, the material we teach, and the expectations we have will influence our students for the rest of their lives. That's a significant obligation; it's also a terrific opportunity. Let's make the most of it.

REFERENCES

Adams, M.J. (1990). *Beginning to read: Thinking and learning about print.* Cambridge: MIT Press.

Adams, M.J., Foorman, B.R., Lundberg, I., & Beeler, T. (1998). *Phonemic awareness in young children: A classroom curriculum.* Baltimore: Paul H. Brookes.

Ahmed, S.T., & Lombardino, L.J. (2000). Invented spelling: An assessment and intervention protocol for kindergarten children. *Communication Disorders Quarterly, 22*(1), 19–28. doi: 10.1177/152574010002200104

Allington, R.L. (2009). *What really matters in response to intervention: Research-based designs.* Boston: Pearson Education.

Allington, R.L., & Cunningham, P.M. (1997). *Schools that work: Where all children read and write.* New York: Addison-Wesley.

Anderson, R.C., Hiebert, E.H., Scott, J.A., & Wilkinson, I.A.G. (1985). *Becoming a nation of readers: The report of the Commission on Reading.* Washington, DC: National Institute of Education.

Ashton-Warner, S. (1963). *Teacher.* New York: Simon & Schuster.

Au, K.H. (2000). Literacy instruction for young children of diverse backgrounds. In D.S. Strickland & L.M. Morrow (Eds.), *Beginning reading and writing* (pp. 35–46). New York: Teachers College Press; Newark, DE: International Reading Association.

Beck, I., McKeown, M. & Kucan, L. (2002). *Bringing words to life: Robust vocabulary instruction.* New York: Guilford.

Benson, V., & Cummins, C. (2000). *The power of retelling: Developmental steps for building comprehension.* Bothell, WA: McGraw-Hill.

Betts, E. (1946). *Foundations of reading instruction: With emphasis on differentiated guidance.* New York: American Book.

Biemiller, A. (2004). Teaching vocabulary in the primary grades: Vocabulary instruction needed. In J. Baumann & E. Kame'enui (Eds.), *Vocabulary instruction: Research to practice* (pp. 28–40). New York: Guilford.

Biemiller, A. (2009). Teaching vocabulary: Early, direct and sequential. In M.F. Graves (Ed.), *Essential readings on vocabulary instruction* (pp. 28–34). Newark, DE: International Reading Association.

Bissett, D. (1969). *The amount and effect of recreational reading in selected fifth-grade classes.* Unpublished doctoral dissertation, Syracuse University, Syracuse, NY.

Block, C., & Mangieri, J. (2009). *Exemplary literacy teachers: What schools can do to promote success for all students.* New York: Guilford.

Block, C., Parris, S., & Whiteley, C. (2008). CPMs: A kinesthetic comprehension strategy. *The Reading Teacher, 61*(6), 460–470. doi:10.1598/RT.61.6.3

Bloodgood, J.W. (1999). What's in a name? Children's name writing and literacy acquisition. *Reading Research Quarterly, 34*(3), 342–367. doi:10.1598/RRQ.34.3.5

Boushey, G., & Moser, J. (2006). *The daily five: Fostering literacy independence in the elementary grades.* Portland, ME: Stenhouse.

Bowman, B., Donovan, S., & Burns, P. (2000). *Eager to learn: Educating preschoolers.* Washington, DC: National Academy Press.

Braunger, J., & Lewis, J. (2006). *Building a knowledge base in reading* (2nd ed.). Newark, DE: International Reading Association.

British Columbia Ministry of Education. (2009). *Kindergarten curriculum package.* Retrieved May 27, 2011 from www.bced.gov.bc.ca/irp/curric_grade_packages/grkcurric_req.pdf

Britton, J. (1970). *Language and learning.* Coral Gables, FL: University of Miami Press.

Calkins, L. (2003). *Units of study in primary writing: A yearlong curriculum K-2.* Portsmouth, NH: Heinemann.

Calhoun, E. (1999). *Teaching beginning reading and writing with the pictureword inductive model.* Alexandria, VA: Association for Supervision and Curriculum Development.

Cambourne, B. (1988) *The whole story: Natural learning and the acquisition of literacy.* Auckland, NZ: Ashton Scholastic.

Clarke, L. (1988). Invented versus traditional spelling in first graders' writings: Effects on learning to spell and read. *Research in the Teaching of English, 22*(3), 281–309.

Clay, M.M. (1966). *Emergent reading behaviour.* Unpublished doctoral thesis, University of Auckland, New Zealand.

Clay, M.M. (1967). The reading behaviour of five-year-old children: A research report. *New Zealand Journal of Educational Studies, 2*(1), 11–31.

Clay, M.M. (1975). *What did I write? Beginning writing behaviour.* Portsmouth, NH: Heinemann.

Clay, M.M. (1991). *Becoming literate: The construction of inner control.* Portsmouth, NH: Heinemann.

Clay, M.M. (1993). *Reading recovery: A guidebook for teachers in training.* Portsmouth, NH: Heinemann.

Cochran-Smith, M. (1984). *The making of a reader.* Norwood, NJ: Albex.

Collins, K. (2008). Supporting children's book choice. In K. Szymusiak, F. Sibberson, & L. Koch (Eds.), *Beyond leveled books: Early and transitional readers in grades K-5* (2nd ed., pp. 72–74). Portland, ME: Stenhouse.

Common Core State Standards Initiative. (2010a). *Key points in the English language arts.* Retrieved April 1, 2011, from www.corestandards.org/about-the-standards/key-points-in-english-language-arts

Common Core State Standards Initiative. (2010b). *Common Core State Standards for English language arts & literacy in history/social studies, science, and technical subjects.* Washington, DC: National Governors Association Center for Best Practices and the Council of Chief State School Officers. Retrieved May 27, 2011, from www.corestandards.org/assets/CCSSI_ELA Standards.pdf

Cunningham, P. (1991). *Phonics they use: Words for reading and writing.* New York: HarperCollins.

Cunningham, P., & Allington, R. (2007). *Classrooms that work: They can all read and write.* New York: Addison Wesley.

Cunningham, A., & Stanovich, K. (1997). Early reading acquisition and its relation to reading experience and ability 10 years later. *Developmental Psychology, 33*(6), 934–945.

DiCesare, K. (2008). Organizing book baskets: Letting kids in on the plan. In K. Szymusiak, F. Sibberson, & L. Koch (Eds.), *Beyond leveled books: Supporting early and transitional readers in grades K–5* (2nd ed., pp. 40–50). Portland, ME: Stenhouse.

Dickinson, D.K. (1989). Effects of a shared reading program on one Head Start language and literacy environment. In J.B. Allen & J.M. Mason (Eds.), *Risk makers, risk takers, risk breakers: Reducing the risks* (pp. 125–153). Portsmouth, NH: Heinemann.

Dickinson, D.K., Golinkoff, R., & Hirsh-Pasek, K. (2010). Speaking out for language: Why language is central to reading development. *Educational Researcher, 39*(4), 305–310. doi:10.3102/0013189X10370204

Dickinson, D.K., & Smith, M.W. (1994). Long-term effects of preschool teachers' book readings on low-income children's vocabulary and story comprehension. *Reading Research Quarterly, 29*(2), 104–122. doi:10.2307/747807

Diller, D. (2003). *Literacy work stations: Making centers work.* Portland, ME: Stenhouse.

Doake, D. (1988). *Reading begins at birth.* Richmond Hill, ON: Scholastic.

Duke, N.K. (2000a). 3-6 minutes per day: The scarcity of informational texts in first grade. *Reading Research Quarterly, 35*(2), 202–224. doi:10.1598/RRQ.35.2.1

Duke, N.K. (2000b). Print environments and experiences offered to first-grade students in very low- and very high-SES school districts. *Reading Research Quarterly, 35*(4), 456–458. doi:10.1598/RRQ.35.4.1

Durkin, D. (1966). *Children who read early.* New York: Teachers College Press.

Ehri, L. (1991). Development of the ability to read words. In R. Barr, M. Kamil, P. Mosenthal, & P.D. Pearson (Eds.), *Learning to read: Basic research and its implications* (pp. 57–74). Hillsdale, NJ: Erlbaum.

Elicker, J., & Mathur, S. (1997). What do they do all day? Comprehensive evaluation of a full-day kindergarten, *Early Childhood Research Quarterly, 12*(4), 459–480.

Fawson, P., & Reutzel, R. (2000). But I only have a basal: Implementing guided reading in early grades. *The Reading Teacher, 54*(1), 84–98.

Feldgus, I., & Cardonick, I. (1999). *Kidwriting: A systematic approach to phonics, journals, and writing workshop.* New York: The Wright Group.

Fielding, L., Wilson, P., & Anderson, R. (1986). A new focus on free reading: The role of trade books in reading instruction. In T. Raphael (Ed.), *The contexts of school-based literacy* (pp. 149–160). New York: Random House.

Fisher, D., Flood, J., Lapp, D., & Frey, N. (2004). Interactive read-alouds: Is there a common set of implementation practices? *The Reading Teacher, 58*(1), 8–17. doi:10.1598/RT.58.1.1

Forester, A.D., & Reinhard, M. (1989). *The learner's way.* Winnipeg, MB: Peguis.

Foulin, J. (2005). Why is letter-name knowledge such a good predictor of learning to read? *Reading and Writing: An Interdisciplinary Journal, 18*(2), 129–155.

Fountas, I., & Pinnell, G.S. (1996). *Guided reading: Good first teaching for all children.* Portsmouth, NH: Heinemann.

Fountas, I., & Pinnell, G. (2002). *Phonics lessons: Letters, words, and how they work, grade K.* Portsmouth, NH: Heinemann.

Fractor, J., Woodruff, M., Martinez, M. & Teale, W. (1993). Let's not miss opportunities to promote voluntary reading: Classroom libraries in the elementary school. *The Reading Teacher, 46*(6), 476–484.

Gallagher, K. (2009). *Readicide: How schools are killing reading and what you can do about it.* Portland, ME: Stenhouse.

Gambrell, L.B., & Dromsky, A. (2000). Fostering reading comprehension. In D.S. Strickland & L.M. Morrow (Eds.), *Beginning reading and writing* (pp. 143–154). New York: Teachers College Press; Newark, DE: International Reading Association.

Goswami, U., & Bryant, P. (1990). *Phonological skills and learning to read.* Mahwah, NJ: Erlbaum.

Graves, D. (1983). *Writing: Teachers and children at work.* Portsmouth, NH: Heinemann.

Graves, M. (Ed.). (2009). *Essential readings on vocabulary instruction.* Newark, DE: International Reading Association.

Haney, M., Bissonnette, V., & Behnken, K. (2003). The relationship among name writing and early literacy skills in kindergarten children. *Child Study Journal, 33*(2), 99–115.

Hanson, R.A., & Farrell, D. (1995). The long-term effects on high school seniors of learning to read in kindergarten. *Reading Research Quarterly, 30*(4), 908–933.

Harste, J., Woodward, V., & Burke, C. (1984). *Language stories and literacy lessons.* Portsmouth, NH: Heinemann.

Hart, B., & Risley, T. (1995). *Meaningful differences in the everyday experience of young American children.* Baltimore: Paul H. Brookes.

Hatch, J.A. (2005). *Teaching in the new kindergarten.* Clifton Park, NY: Thomson Delmar Learning.

Hayes, D.P., & Ahrens, M. (1988). Vocabulary simplification for children: A special case of 'motherese'? *Journal of Child Language, 15*(2), 395–410.

Heath, S.B. (1983). *Ways with words: Language life and work in communities and classrooms.* Cambridge, UK: Cambridge University Press.

Hickman, J. (1981). A new perspective on response to literature: Research in an elementary school setting. *Research in the Teaching of English, 15*(4), 343–354.

Hiebert, E.H., & Raphael, T.E. (1998). *Early literacy instruction.* Fort Worth, TX: Harcourt Brace.

Holdaway, D. (1979). *The foundations of literacy.* Sydney, NSW, Australia: Ashton Scholastic.

Iaquinta, A. (2006). Guided reading: A research-based response to the challenges of early reading instruction. *Early Childhood Education Journal, 33*(6), 413–418. doi:10.1007/s10643-006-0074-2

International Reading Association. (1997). *The role of phonics in reading instruction* (Position statement). Newark, DE: Author.

International Reading Association. (1998). *Phonemic awareness and the teaching of reading. A position statement from the Board of Directors of the International Reading Association.* Newark, DE: Author.

International Reading Association & National Association for the Education of Young Children. (1998). Learning to read and write: Developmentally appropriate practices for children. *The Reading Teacher, 52*(2) 193–216.

Jacobson, J. (2010). *No more "I'm done!": Fostering independent writers in the primary grades.* Portland, ME: Stenhouse.

Johnson, T.D., & Louis, D.R. (1987). *Literacy through literature.* Richmond Hill, ON: Scholastic.

Jones, C.D., Retuzel, D.R., & Fargo, J.D. (2010). Comparing two methods of writing instruction: Effects on kindergarten students' reading skills. *Journal of Educational Research, 103*(5), 327–341.

Joshi, R.M. (2005). Vocabulary: A critical component of comprehension. *Reading and Writing Quarterly: Overcoming Learning Difficulties, 21*(3), 209–219.

Juel, C., Biancarosa, G., Coker, D., & Deffes, R. (2003). Walking with Rosie: A cautionary tale of early reading instruction. *Educational Leadership, 60*(7), 12–18.

Juel, C., & Deffes, R. (2004). Making words stick. *Educational Leadership: What Research Says About Reading, 61*(6), 30–34.

Justice, L.M., & Pullen, P.C. (2003). Promising interventions for promoting emergent literacy skills: Three evidence-based approaches. *Topics in Early Childhood Special Education, 23*(3), 99–113.

Kosanovich, M., Ladinsky, K., Nelson, L., & Torgensen, J. (2006). *Differentiated reading instruction: Small group alternative lesson structures for* all *students.* Tallahassee: Florida Center for Reading Research. Retrieved May 19, 2011, from www.fcrr.org/assessment/pdf/smallgroupalternativelessonstructures.pdf

LaBerge, D., & Samuels, S.J. (1974). Toward a theory of automatic information processing in reading. *Cognitive Psychology, 6*(2) 293–323. doi:10.1016/0010-0285(74)90015-2

Langer, J. (1996). *Envisioning literature: Literary understanding and literature instruction.* New York: Teachers College Press.

Lapp, D., Flood, J., & Roser, N. (2000). Still standing: Timeless strategies for teaching the language arts. In D.S. Strickland & L.M. Morrow (Eds.), *Beginning reading and writing* (pp. 183–193). New York: Teachers College Press; Newark, DE: International Reading Association.

Lehr, S. (1988). The child's developing sense of theme as a response to literature. *Reading Research Quarterly, 23*(3), 337–357.

Marcon, R. (2002). Moving up the grades: Relationship between preschool model and later school success. *Early Childhood Research and Practice, 4*(1). Retrieved April 16, 2011, from ecrp.uiuc.edu/v4n1/marcon.html

Martinez, M., & Roser, N. (1985). Read it again: The value of repeated readings during storytime. *The Reading Teacher, 38*(8), 782–786.

Martinez, M., Roser, N., & Dooley, C. (2003). Young children's literacy meaning making. In N. Hall, J. Larson, & J. Marsh. (Eds.), *Handbook of early childhood literacy* (pp. 222–234). London: SAGE.

Martinez, M., & Teale, W. (1987). The ins and outs of a kindergarten writing program. *The Reading Teacher, 40*(4), 444–451.

Martinez, M., & Teale, W. (1988). Reading in a kindergarten classroom library. *The Reading Teacher, 41*(6), 568–572.

Massey, S. (2004). Teacher-child conversation in the preschool classroom. *Early Childhood Education Journal, 31*(4), 227–231. doi:10.1023/B:ECEJ.0000024113.69141.23

McCarrier, A., Pinnell, G.S., & Fountas, I. (2000). *Interactive writing: How language and literacy come together.* Portsmouth, NH: Heinemann.

McGee, L.M., & Richgels, D.J. (1989). "K is Kristen's": Learning the alphabet from a child's perspective. *The Reading Teacher, 43*(3), 216–225.

McGee, L.M., & Richgels, D.J. (2003). *Designing early literacy programs: Strategies for at-risk preschool and kindergarten children.* New York: Guilford.

McGee, L.M., & Schickedanz, J.A. (2007). Repeated interactive read-alouds in preschool and kindergarten. *The Reading Teacher, 60*(8), 742–751. doi:10.1598/RT.60.8.4

McGill-Franzen, A. (2006). *Kindergarten literacy: Matching assessment and instruction in kindergarten.* New York: Scholastic.

Miller, L. (1998). Literacy interactions through environmental print. In R. Campbell (Ed.), *Facilitating preschool literacy* (pp. 100–118). Newark, DE: International Reading Association.

Morphett, M., & Washburne, C. (1931). When should children begin to read? *The Elementary School Journal, 31*(7), 496–503.

Morrow, L.M. (1985). Retelling stories: A strategy for improving young children's comprehension, concept of story structure, and oral language complexity. *The Elementary School Journal, 85*(5), 646–661. doi:10.1086/461427

Morrow, L.M. (1988). Young children's responses to one-on-one story readings in school settings. *Reading Research Quarterly, 23*(1), 89–107.

Morrow, L.M. (1991). Promoting voluntary reading. In J. Jenson, D. Lapp, J. Flood, & J. Squire (Eds.), *Handbook of research on teaching the English language arts* (pp. 681–690). New York: Macmillan.

Morrow, L.M. (1997). *The literacy center: Contexts for reading and writing.* York, ME: Stenhouse.

Morrow, L.M., & Asbury, E. (2003). Current practices in early literacy development. In L.M. Morrow, L.B. Gambrell, &, M. Pressley (Eds.), *Best practices in literacy instruction* (2nd ed., pp. 43–63). New York: Guilford.

Morrow, L.M., O'Connor, E.M., & Smith, J.K. (1990). Effects of a story reading program on the literacy development of at-risk kindergarten children. *Journal of Reading Behavior, 22*(3), 255–275.

Morrow, L.M., & Rand, M.K. (1991). Promoting literacy during play by designing early childhood classroom environments. *The Reading Teacher, 44*(6), 396–402.

Nation, K., & Hulme, C. (1997). Phonemic segmentation, not onset-rime segmentation, predicts early reading and spelling skills. *Reading Research Quarterly, 32*(2), 154–167. doi:10.1598/RRQ.32.2.2

National Association for the Education of Young Children. (1986). A position statement on developmentally appropriate practices in early childhood programs serving children from birth through age eight.

National Association for the Education of Young Children. (2009). *Developmentally appropriate practice in early childhood programs serving children from birth through age 8* (Position statement). Washington, DC: Author. Retrieved May 5, 2011, from www.naeyc.org/files/naeyc/file/positions/position%20statement%20Web.pdf

National Early Literacy Panel. (2008). *Developing early literacy: Report of the National Early Literacy Panel.* National Institute for Literacy. Retrieved May 6, 2011, from lincs.ed.gov/publications/pdf/NELPReport09.pdf

National Institute of Child Health and Human Development. (2000). *Report of the National Reading Panel. Teaching children to read: An evidence-based assessment of the scientific research literature on reading and its implications for reading instruction: Reports of the subgroups.* Washington, DC: U.S. Government Printing Office.

National KIDS COUNT Program. (2009). *Children in poverty (Percent)—2009.* Baltimore: Annie E. Casey Foundation. Retrieved June 13, 2011, datacenter.kidscount.org/data/acrossstates/Rankings.aspx?ind=43

National Research Council. (2001). *Eager to learn: Educating our preschoolers.* Washington, DC: National Academy Press.

National Writing Project. (2002). Thinking about the reading/writing connection with David Pearson. *The Voice, 7*(2). Retrieved November 26, 2010, from www.nwp.org/cs/public/print/resource/329

Neuman, S.B., & Celano, D. (2001). Access to print in low-income and middle-income communities: An ecological study of four neighborhoods. *Reading Research Quarterly, 36*(1), 8–26. doi:10.1598/RRQ.36.1.1

Neuman, S.B., Copple, C., & Bredekamp, S. (2000). *Learning to read and write: Developmentally appropriate practices for young children.* Washington, DC: National Association for the Education of Young Children.

Neuman, S.B., & Roskos, K.A. (1992). Literacy objects as cultural tools: Effects on children's literacy behaviors in play. *Reading Research Quarterly, 27*(3), 203–225.

Neuman, S.B., & Roskos, K.A. (1998). *Children achieving: Best practices in early literacy.* Newark, DE: International Reading Association.

Obiakor, F. (2006). *Multicultural special education: Culturally responsive teaching.* Upper Saddle River, NJ: Merrill.

Oczkus, L. (2004). *Super six comprehension strategies: 35 lessons and more for reading success.* Norwood, MA: Christopher-Gordon.

O'Reilly, J., & Yau, M. (2009). 2008 parent census, kindergarten–grade 6: System overview and detailed findings. Toronto, ON, Canada: Toronto District School Board.

Owocki, G. (1999). *Literacy through play.* Portsmouth, NH: Heinemann.

Parkes, B. (2000). *Read it again! Revisiting shared reading.* Portland, ME: Stenhouse.

Partridge, M. (1991). *The effects of daily opportunities to draw and write on kindergarten children's ability to represent phonemes in their spelling inventions.* Paper presented at the Annual Meeting of the National Association for the Education of Young Children, Denver, CO.

Pearson, P.D., & Gallagher, M.C. (1983). The instruction of reading comprehension. *Contemporary Educational Psychology, 8*(3), 317-344.

Peterson, M.E., & Haines, L.P. (1992). Orthographic training with kindergarten children: Effects of analogy use, phonemic segmentation and letter-sound knowledge. In C. Weaver (Ed.), *Reconsidering a balanced approach to literacy* (pp. 159–180). Urbana, IL: National Council of Teachers of English.

Piaget, J. (1929). *The child's conception of the world.* New York: Harcourt Brace Jovanovich.

Plucker, J. et al. (2004). *The effects of full day versus half day kindergarten: Review and analysis of national and Indiana data.* Center for Evaluation and Education Policy. Retrieved May 5, 2011 from www.doe.state.in.us/primetime/pdf/fulldaykreport.pdf

Prior, J., & Gerard, M. (2004). *Environmental print in the classroom.* Newark, DE: International Reading Association.

Puckett, M.B., & Diffily, D. (2004). *Teaching young children: An introduction to the early childhood profession.* Clifton Park, NY: Delmar Cengage.

Reutzel, D.R., Oda, L.K., & Moore, B.H. (1989). Developing print awareness: The effects of three instructional approaches on kindergarteners' print awareness, reading readiness, and word reading. *Journal of Reading Behavior, 21*(3), 197–217.

Richardson, J. (2009). *The next step in guided reading: Focused assessments and targeted lessons for helping every student become a better reader.* New York: Scholastic.

Robinson, R., & McKenna, M. (2007). *Issues and trends in literacy education.* Boston: Allyn & Bacon.

Rog, L.J. (2001). *Early literacy instruction in kindergarten.* Newark, DE: International Reading Association.

Rog, L.J. (2006). *Marvelous minilessons for teaching beginning writing, K–3.* Newark, DE: International Reading Association.

Roskos, K.A. (1995). Creating places for play with print. In J.F Christie, K.A. Roskos, B.J. Enz, C. Vukelich, & S.B. Neuman (Eds.), *Readings for linking literacy and play* (pp. 8–17). Newark, DE: International Reading Association.

Rubadue, M. (2002). Sharing the pen. *Teaching pre-K–8, 32*(6), 58.

Russell, J.L. (2011). From child's garden to academic press: The role of shifting institutional logics in redefining kindergarten education. *American Educational Research Journal, 48*(2), 236–267.

Scanlon, D., Anderson, K., & Sweeney, J. (2010). *Early intervention for reading difficulties: The interactive strategies approach.* New York: Guilford.

Schickedanz, J. (2004). A framework and suggested guidelines for prekindergarten content standards. *The Reading Teacher, 58*(1), 95–97.

Sénéchal, M., & Cornell, E.H. (1993). Vocabulary acquisition through shared reading experiences. *Reading Research Quarterly, 28*(4), 360–375.

Sipe, L. (2000). The construction of literary understanding by first and second graders in oral response to picture storybook read-alouds. *Reading Research Quarterly, 35*(2), 252–275.

Slocumb, P.D., & Payne, R.K. (2000). *Removing the mask: Giftedness in poverty.* Highlands, TX: RFT.

Smolkin, L. (2000). How will diversity affect literacy in the next millennium? Response by Laura Smolkin. *Reading Research Quarterly, 35*(4), 549–550.

Smolkin, L.B., & Donovan, C.A. (2003). Supporting comprehension acquisition for emerging and struggling readers: The interactive information book read-aloud. *Exceptionality, 11*(1), 25–38. doi:10.1207/S15327035EX1101_3

Snell, C.A. (2007). *The impact of daily writing on kindergarten students' phonemic awareness.* *DAI, 68*(04). (UMI No. 3261224)

Snow, C.E., Burns, M.S., & Griffin, P. (1998). *Preventing reading difficulties in young children.* Washington, DC: National Academy Press.

Southall, M. (2009). *Differentiated small-group reading lessons.* New York: Scholastic.

Stanovich, K. (1994). Romance and reality. *The Reading Teacher, 47*(4), 280–291.

Stead, T. (2006). *Reality checks: Teaching reading comprehension with nonfiction K-5.* Portland, ME: Stenhouse.

Stipek, D., Feiler, R., Daniels, D., & Milburn, S. (1995). Effects of different instructional approaches on young children's achievement and motivation. *Child Development, 66*(1), 209–223.

Strickland, D.S. (2000). Classroom intervention strategies: Supporting the literacy development of young learners at risk. In D.S. Strickland & L.M. Morrow (Eds.), *Beginning reading and writing* (pp. 99–110). New York: Teachers College Press; Newark, DE: International Reading Association.

Strickland, D. (2008). "When DAP meets GAP: Promoting peaceful coexistence between developmentally appropriate practice & the need to address the achievement gap." Retrieved October 201, 2010, from oldweb.naeyc.org/dap/doc/strickland.ppt

Strickland, D., & Feeley, J. (2003). Development in the elementary school years. In J. Flood, D. Lapp, J. Squire, & J. Jenson (Eds.), *Handbook of research on teaching the English* language (2nd ed., pp. 339–356). Newark, DE: International Reading Association; Urbana, IL: National Council of Teachers of English.

Sulzby, E. (1985). Children's emergent reading of favorite storybooks: A developmental study. *Reading Research Quarterly, 20*(4), 458–481. doi:10.1598/RRQ.20.4.4

Sulzby, E., Teale, W.H., & Kamberelis, G. (1989). Emergent writing in the classroom: Home and school connections. In D.S. Strickland & L.M. Morrow (Eds.), *Emerging literacy: Young children learn to read and write* (pp. 147–159). Newark, DE: International Reading Association.

Teale, W.H., & Yokota, J. (2000). Foundations of the early literacy curriculum. In D.S. Strickland & L.M. Morrow (Eds.), *Beginning reading and writing* (pp. 3–21). New York: Teachers College Press; Newark, DE: International Reading Association.

Treiman, R., & Broderick, V. (1998). What's in a name: Children's knowledge about the letters in their own names. *Journal of Experimental Child Psychology, 70*(2), 97–116.

Tyner, B. (2004). *Small-group reading instruction: A differentiated teaching model for beginning and struggling readers.* Newark, DE: International Reading Association.

Van Horn, M.L., Karlin, E.O., Ramey, S.L., Aldridge, J., & Snyder, S.W. (2005). Effects of developmentally appropriate practices on children's development: A review of research and discussion of methodological and analytic issues. *Elementary School Journal, 105*(4), 325–351.

Vygotsky, L.S. (1978). *Mind in society: The development of higher psychological processes* (M. Cole, V. John-Steiner, S. Scribner, & E. Souberman, Eds. & Trans.). Cambridge, MA: Harvard University Press.

Walston, J., & West, J. (2004). *Full-day and half-day kindergarten in the United States: Findings from the Early Childhood Longitudinal Study, Kindergarten Class of 1998–99* (NCES-2004-078). U.S. Department of Education. National Center for Education Statistics. Washington, DC: U.S. Government Printing Office.

Wasik, B. (2010). What teachers can do to promote preschoolers' vocabulary development: Strategies from an effective language and literacy professional development coaching model. *The Reading Teacher, 63*(8), 621–633.

Welsch, J. (2008). Playing within and beyond the story: Encouraging book-related pretend play. *The Reading Teacher, 62*(2), 138–148.

Wigfield, A. (1997). Children's motivations for reading and reading engagement. In J.T. Guthrie & A. Wigfield (Eds.), *Reading engagement: Motivating readers through integrated instruction* (pp. 14–33). Newark, DE: International Reading Association.

Wollons, R.L. (Ed). (2000). *Kindergartens and cultures: The global diffusion of an idea.* New Haven, CT: Yale University Press.

Youngquist, J., & Pataray-Ching, J. (2004). Revisiting "play": Analyzing and articulating acts of inquiry. *Early Childhood Education Journal, 31*(3), 171–178.

Zill, N., & West, J. (2000). Entering kindergarten: Findings from the Condition of Education 2000 (NCES 2001-035). National Center for Education Statistics. Retrieved April 28, 2010, from nces.ed.gov/pubs2001/2001035.pdf

CHILDREN'S BOOK REFERENCES

Ahlberg, J., & Ahlberg, A. (1986). *The jolly postman.* Boston: Little, Brown.

Aliki. (1996). *Hello! Good-bye!* New York: Greenwillow.

Alpers, J. (2005). *T is for tortilla: A southwestern alphabet book.* Santa Fe, NM: Azro.

Barrett, J. (2001). *Things that are most in the world.* New York: Atheneum.

Borden, L. (1989). *Caps, hats, socks, and mittens: A book about the four seasons.* New York: Scholastic.

Brown, L. (2006). *How to be.* New York: HarperCollins.

Brown, M.W. (1999). *The important book.* New York: HarperCollins.

Cronin, D. (2003). *Diary of a worm.* New York: HarperCollins.

dePaola, T. (1975). *Strega nona.* New York: Simon & Schuster.

Dobson, C. (2003). *Pizza counting.* Watertown, MA: Charlesbridge.

Eastman, P.D. (1960). *Are you my mother?* New York: Random House.

Ehlert, L. (1993). *Eating the alphabet.* New York: Red Wagon.

Feldman, E. (1996). *Birthdays! Celebrating life around the world.* Mahwah, NJ: Bridgewater.

Henkes, K. (1991). *Chrysanthemum.* New York: Greenwillow.

Henkes, K. (1993). *Owen.* New York: HarperCollins.

Henkes, K. (1996). *Lily's purple plastic purse.* New York: Greenwillow.

Hill, M. (2002). *Let's make pizza.* New York: Children's Press.

Kitamura, S. (1992). *From Acorn to Zoo and everything in between in alphabetical order.* New York: Farrar, Straus & Giroux.

Martin, B., Jr. (1996). *Brown bear, Brown bear, what do you see?* New York: Henry Holt.

McMullan, K., & McMullan, J. (2006). *I stink!* New York: HarperCollins.

Munsch, R. (1985). *Mortimer.* Toronto, ON, Canada: Annick.

Munsch, R. (1992). *The paper bag princess.* Toronto, ON, Canada: Annick.

Neitzel, S. (1989). *The jacket I wear in the snow.* New York: Greenwillow.

Numeroff, L. (1985). If you give a mouse a cookie. New York: Harper & Row.

Older, E. (2000). *My two grandmothers.* San Diego, CA: Harcourt.

Pallotta, J. (1993). *The icky bug alphabet book.* Watertown, MA: Charlesbridge.

Rosenthal, A.K. (2005). *Little pea.* San Francisco: Chronicle.

Shoulders, M., & Shoulders, D. (2006). *D is for drum: A Native American alphabet.* Sleeping Bear.

Soto, G. (1996). *Too many tamales.* New York: Putnam.

Stead, T. (2002). *Should there be zoos? A persuasive text.* New York: Mondo.

Thornhill, J. (1988). *The wildlife ABC: A nature alphabet.* Toronto, ON, Canada: Grey de Pencier.

Tolhurst, M. (1991). *Somebody and the three Blairs.* New York: Orchard.

Ward, C. (1992). *Cookie's week.* New York: Putnam.

Watt, M. (2007). *Scaredy squirrel makes a friend.* Toronto, ON, Canada: Kids Can.

Wyeth, S.D. (2002). *Something beautiful.* New York: Dragonfly.

Yolen, J. (1987). *Owl moon.* New York: Philomel.

INDEX

Note. Page numbers followed by *f* and *t* indicate figures and tables, respectively.

reading fingers, 95

reading phones, 93, 93*f*

reading readiness, 8

Reinhard, M., 107

reproducible books, 111

rereading, 60, 100–101

research: on emergent literacy, 9–11; on rereading, 60; and vocabulary instruction, 56–57

Response to Intervention (RTI), 162

retelling, 70–71; stages in, 107–108

Retelling Ribbon, 70–71

Reutzel, D.R., 86

review, and play, 32, 33*f*

Richardson, J., 136

Richgels, D.J., 22, 48

rimes, 17, 52

Risley, T., 47, 55

Robinson, R., 60

Rog, L.J., 114

Roser, N., 60, 103

Roskos, K.A., 10, 35, 41

routines: learning, 87; for name study, 143–145

RTI. *See* Response to Intervention

Rubadue, M., 124

S

Samuels, S.J., 151

scaffolding, 5, 118

Scanlon, D., 152

Schickedanz, J., 6, 48, 60, 63, 66

Scott, J.A., 59

self-monitoring, 100

Sénéchal C, 17

Shape-Go Map, 70, 71*f*

shared reading, 73–83, 74*f*; and word play, 155–156, 156*f*

shared writing, 81, 116–118

sharing time, 134–135, 134*f*

Show What You Know game, 76

shower curtain games, 152, 153*f*

sight word tally, 153

Sipe, L., 62–63

sliders, 98, 100*f,* 151

Slocumb, P.D., 159–160

small-group reading instruction, 84–102

Smith, J.K., 60

Smith, M.W., 62, 83

Smolkin, L., 61, 159

Snell, C.A., 126

Snow, C.E., 16

Snyder, S.W., 12

sound sorting, 55

Southall, M., 153

standards, kindergarten literacy, 23–24

Stanovich, K., 17, 52, 161

Stead, T., 67

Sticky Dot Details, 116

Stipek, D., 12

Strickland, D., 14, 125, 162

Sulzby, E., 5, 28–29, 107, 136, 138

Sweeney, J., 152

syllables, 17, 52

syntax, 49

T

talk to your neighbor (TTYN), 66

Teach Three Words, 56–57, 65*f,* 69

teaching: changed understandings of, 4–7; and classroom, 42–43; developmentally appropriate practice and, 10–15; intentional, 13–14

Teale, W., 28–29, 60, 71, 77, 103–104, 138, 140

team, for small-group instruction, 88

text matching, 78

text selection: for classroom library, 104–105; for emergent readers, 106–107; for independent readers, 105–107; for read-alouds, 60–62; for shared reading, 75

Text Talk, 56, 69

think-aloud prompts, 68–69

tickle trunk, 40

Tolhurst, M., 53, 109

tools, for guided reading, 95

topics, for writing, 114, 130–131